MW01138891

ON WORDS

ON WORDS

INSIGHT INTO HOW OUR WORDS WORK — AND DON'T

PAULA LaRocque
AUTHOR OF THE BOOK ON WRITING

Marion Street Press, Inc.
Oak Park, Illinois

Cover design by Ed Avis

ISBN: 1-933338-20-2
ISBN-13: 978-1-933338-20-0
Printed in U.S.A.
Printing 10 9 8 7 6 5 4 3 2 1

Marion Street Press, Inc.
PO Box 2249
Oak Park, IL 60303
866-443-7987
www.marionstreetpress.com

To Paul, as always
And to Carol, Mark, and Paul II

Also by **PAULA LaRocque:**

THE BOOK ON WRITING: THE ULTIMATE GUIDE TO WRITING WELL
A step-by-step primer on becoming a fantastic writer. Loaded with examples of great writing.

Marion Street Press, Inc., $18.95, 240 pages, ISBN 0966517695

CHAMPIONSHIP WRITING: 50 WAYS TO IMPROVE YOUR WRITING
A fun-to-read guide to good writing in 50 quick lessons. The chapters originated from columns LaRocque wrote for QUILL magazine.

Marion Street Press, Inc., $18.95, 206 pages, ISBN 0966517636

Available at bookstores and online at www.marionstreetpress.com

PAULA LaRocque
Biography

Paula LaRocque is a communications consultant who has conducted writing workshops for hundreds of media, government, academic, and business groups in the United States, Canada, and Europe. She was assistant managing editor, writing coach, and frequent columnist at *The Dallas Morning News* from 1981 through 2001. She also has been consultant for the Associated Press, the Drehscheibe Institute in Bonn, and the European Stars & Stripes in Germany.

From 1971 to 1981, she taught technical writing at Western Michigan University's School of Engineering, and creative or journalistic writing at Texas A&M, Southern Methodist, and Texas Christian universities.

She is a columnist for *Quill* magazine, and her commentaries are aired regularly on National Public Radio in Dallas. She is author of *The Book on Writing: The Ultimate Guide to Writing Well*, and *Championship Writing: 50 Ways to Improve Your Writing* (Marion Street Press, Inc.), and is at work on her first novel, a mystery.

Paula was elected to the Associated Press Managing Editors Executive Board in 1998, and in 2001 she received that organization's Meritorious Service Award for exemplary contribution to journalism.

She earned a Bachelor of Arts degree *Summa Cum Laude* from Western Michigan University and a Master of Arts degree from the same school.

CONTENTS

PART 1: WORDS AND CULTURE

PART 2: WORDS AS WORDS

PART 3: WORDS AND CALENDAR

PART 4: WORDS AND MEDIA

SECTION 5: WORDS AND MECHANICS

Author's Note

The columns in this collection originally appeared in this or a slightly different form in *Quill*, the Society of Professional Journalists' magazine; in my "Words Matter" column in *The Dallas Morning News*; or were broadcast on Dallas' National Public Radio station, KERA.

The columns constitute a wide range of topics but in one way or the other are about words and the way we use (or misuse) them. They're loosely organized into five parts: Words & Culture, Words & the Media, Words as Words, Words & the Calendar, and Words & Mechanics. Those sections are in no way comprehensive — I avoided material that might repeat or overlap significantly with material in my earlier books (*The Book on Writing: The Ultimate Guide to Writing Well*, and another collection of columns, *Championship Writing: 50 Ways to Improve Your Writing*). The section on mechanics, particularly, could be a volume in itself, but I've discussed grammatical, structural, and other mechanical matters thoroughly in my earlier works.

I sincerely hope you find within these covers something entertaining or enlightening, or both.

Paula LaRocque
Arlington, Texas

PART ONE

WORDS AND CULTURE

CHAPTER 1

LANGUAGE LIMITS
LIMIT OUR WORLD

The saying that perception is everything is often true of the language. Recently, I bought a pair of slacks that seemed an indeterminate color in the store's indirect lighting.

"What color is this?" I asked the clerk and, after a moment's study, she said, "Light black."

I realized instantly that I had no such color category. To me, when black wasn't dark enough to be black, it was gray. And gray was what I needed, so I took the pants home, where their color again seemed uncertain.

"These new gray pants?" I said to my husband. "I think they're brown."

He looked at them. "No," he said. "They're not brown. And they're not gray. They're . . . black. Well, not black black, but mostly black. Or sort of black."

I saw he didn't have a name for the color either. I looked at the small print on the tag hanging from the waistband. It said: "Light Black."

So I now have a new color category. Light black is the color of a deep river on a sunless day — not gray or black or brown or green, but a murky shade of all those. I will recognize that color when I see it again. It has a name and, to me, it will be a "real" color.

Color is interesting to linguists who study language differences in different cultures. Such study can illumine the idea that since we think in words, we can think only about what we have words for — or, as Ludwig Wittgenstein put it: "The limits of my language are the limits of my world." Ronald Reagan once played upon this idea by announcing that the Russians have no word for freedom. (He was wrong, however, and those who knew promptly pointed out that the Russian word for freedom was *svoboda*.)

How we perceive color and what we call it is valuable to language study because color is not an abstract idea — it's a physical reality. Unless we're color-blind, you and I should see basically the same thing when we look at the color spectrum. Yet, our culture identifies six bands of colors in the spectrum — and many shades within those primary bands — while other cultures identify different numbers and divisions. We see red, orange, yellow, green, blue, and purple. But, as Peter Farb writes in his book *Word Play*, the Shona of Rhodesia see three main bands in the spectrum: red and orange form one band, yellow and green a second, and purple and red a third. The Bassa of Liberia see two basic divisions in the spectrum — cool and warm. Peter Farb also writes of languages that have only two color terms — black and white — and concludes that cultures develop more words for different colors as those cultures grow more complex.

We have plenty of colors in our complex culture and, as we saw with "light black," if we need another, we just invent it. Then we give it a name, something associative usually, to help us identify and recall it — "celery," say, or "ruby." If the name sticks and correctly calls that color to our minds, it becomes a "real" color, in our minds. Our perception has widened with our spectrum.

An item in a catalog is available in these colors: apache, jungle, amazon, dune, safari, cloud, twilight, nile. This is the naming game in action — finding a non-color name to suggest color — and it demands broad perspective.

As we've seen, though, perceiving color — like perceiving many things — can also reveal a narrow perspective. Our crayon boxes once held a rosy beige crayon called "flesh." The catalog I just mentioned shows pale beige tights called "nude," and three shades of face powder: alabaster, ivory, and pearl. In these names we see a failure of the imagination, a suggestion of what Wittgenstein meant when he said, "The limits of my language are the limits of my world."

Many color names should successfully bring rosy beige

to mind, but "flesh" isn't one of them — any more than pale beige describes all nudes, or alabaster, ivory, and pearl all faces. Does it matter? It does. If I were a person of color — and especially if I were a child forming my perceptions and identity — it would be hurtful to realize that my own flesh was somehow outside the spectrum.

CHAPTER 2

BARBARIAN

I recently heard a certain politician referred to as a "barbarian." The speaker wasn't referring to savage or cruel behavior, but to the politician's language skills. Most people are passionate about what they consider misuse of the language, and they show it in their own choice of words. One seldom hears such mild reproofs as: *Oh, goodness, his grammar is a bit off-putting.* Or: *My, her pronunciation is quaint, isn't it?*

No. We hear instead: *If he says "irregardless" one more time, I'm going to shoot him.* Or: *If she doesn't stop saying "ax" instead of "ask," I'm going to throw something.*

Our metaphors for language misuse are often violent. We don't say people misuse the language; we say they "maim," "abuse," "massacre," "brutalize" or "butcher" it. That visceral reaction arises in part because our language and our ideas of its proper use are dear to us. A native tongue is of great value to its speakers, who are sensitive to its use even if they themselves are not expert users. Some countries even have ministries of language charged with preserving the purity of the mother tongue.

Maybe that sensitivity is why we so often feel bound to correct others' grammar or usage although we know it might embarrass them. Even if we don't correct, the temptation to do so is strong — sometimes almost a reflex. Let someone say "This is between you and I," and someone else blurts almost without thinking: "between you and *me*."

Whatever the reason, most people have well defined linguistic pet peeves. Occasionally, to be sure, the person with the peeve is wrong — as is the case with the supposed "errors" of the split infinitive, ending sentences with prepositions, or beginning sentences with *and* or *but*. Not one of those practices is wrong, but folks who think so are no less peeved for being mistaken. Instead, they might respond: "Well, OK, it may not be wrong, but I still hate it!"

It's hard to give up a peeve, especially a pet one.

Some of the strongest peeves have to do with speech rather than writing. Many cannot bear to hear the word *nuclear* pronounced "nucular," or *Realtor* pronounced "realator." Others are infuriated by double negatives such as *can't hardly, don't have no, can't do nothing*. Still others go crazy over the repeated use of *you know* or *totally*.

I recently saw a roomful of editors collectively flinch when they heard someone use "antidote" when he meant *anecdote*. A friend says that when he hears *literally* and *figuratively* confused, he stops in his figurative tracks and grits his literal teeth. On my own list of teeth-grinding grotesqueries are "ekcetera" instead of *etcetera*, and "asterick" instead of *asterisk*.

As mentioned elsewhere in this book, many can hardly bear the suffixes "-wise" and "-ize" randomly tacked onto nouns. They have plenty of opportunity to exercise their peeve — one hears that leaden, lengthening syllable everywhere. I recently arrived at a banquet hall to deliver a speech on linguistic grace and precision, and the host announced they were having trouble "microphonewise." A relatively new and despised creation is "incentivize," which means to provide incentives. "Utilize" is an outcast in the land of the peeved.

Being sensitive to the language and scornful of its misuse is nothing new — which takes us back to "barbarian." Long ago, the Latin word *balbus* meant someone who stammered or spoke haltingly. That word passed into Spanish as *bobo* and in turn spawned *booby* or *boob*. And just as we mimic incomprehensible language with the words *blah blah*, the Greeks made fun of what they considered gibberish with the words *bar-bar*. The Greeks were proud of their language, as we all are, and were scornful of those who didn't understand it.

Eventually *bar-bar* came to mean foreign or savage and in time transmuted to *barbaros* and the related *barbarous, barbarism,* and *barbarian.* It's interesting that those words, which mean *uncivilized*, can be traced to a lack of fluency. Apparently, our inherent understanding of being civilized means, in part, the ability to communicate well — not only with grace and accuracy, but also without offense.

CHAPTER 3

CRAZY LABELS

This label is stitched into a side seam of my new tee-shirt:

> MACHINE WASH COLD.
> HANG TO DRY, POSSIBLE
> SHRINKAGE OF 5% WHEN
> WASHED OR DRY CLEAN.

Something's wrong, but what? Should "dry clean" be "dry *cleaned*," meaning the garment can be either laundered or dry-cleaned and that it may shrink a little either way?

Or, more likely, should there be a period after "washed" — meaning the garment can be washed but may shrink, or, alternatively, can be dry cleaned and will not shrink?

Missing period or tense problem — it could go either way. The label has two periods and a comma, though, suggesting that the writer knows there is such a thing as punctuation, even if the comma following "hang to dry" is wrong. The fact that all letters on the label are capitalized doesn't help, either — you can't tell where sentences begin and end.

I washed it. I'm going to dry clean a *tee shirt*? And it shrank a little. About five percent, I'd say.

But that's not my beef.

Why is writing so careless and ill conceived that the simplest communication bewilders even the educated? Sometimes manuals and instructions are written by those who don't know English as a mother tongue, true, and that's bound to cause problems. But this shirt says "Made in U.S.A." Could we then expect periods at the ends of sentences, or upper- and lower-case letters, or correct tense — the way we do it in English — or one sentence per line, at least?

There's no shortage of labeling or packaging bewilderments. A consumer query posted on the British "Plain English" website notes that a certain coffee package reads: "Product of Central America, Colombia, and Tanzania. Packed in Belgium."

"Why," the writer asks, "is this product called '*Italian Blend*'?"

A bag of snack chips carries the proclamation: "You could be a winner! No purchase necessary! Details inside!" Details inside but no purchase necessary? (Steal this bag!)

Or consider this shower cap provided by a hotel. The information printed on the container reads: "Contents: Shower cap. Fits one head." (In case you two thought you were going to get in there together.)

You have to wonder what the makers of a string of Christmas lights was thinking when they provided this label: "For indoor or outdoor use only." (Is there something else?)

Especially entertaining are product warnings. A Michigan group, the Lawsuit Abuse Watch, each year chooses the wackiest warning labels of the year — usually either obvious or ridiculous warnings. Some recent winners:

• A caution on a five-inch fishing device with three steel hooks: "Harmful if swallowed."

• A warning on a 12-inch-high storage rack for compact discs: "Do not use as a ladder."

• Advice on a sled label: "Beware: Sled may develop high speed under certain snow conditions."

• A message on a bottle of drain cleaner: "If you do not understand, or cannot read, all directions, cautions, and warnings, do not use this product."

And here are some other product warnings, gleaned from the Internet, which must have come from equally overprotective legal departments:

• An iron: "Do not iron clothes on body."

• A hairdryer: "Do not use while sleeping."

• A sleep aid: "Warning: May cause drowsiness."

• A Superman costume: "The wearing of this garment does not enable you to fly."

• A jar of peanuts: "Warning: contains nuts."

Some label instructions are less than helpful. A packet of airline nuts reads: "Instructions: open packet, eat nuts." A frozen dinner advises: "Serving suggestion: Defrost." And a frozen dessert has this caution printed on the bottom of the box: "Do not turn upside down." (Too late!)

Those are all entertaining, but if I were on that committee to pick the wackiest warning labels of the year, my money would be on this one, accompanying a chainsaw: "Do not attempt to stop chain with your hands or genitals."

CHAPTER 4

MONDEGREENS

Most new television sets offer the hearing-impaired an on-screen text of a speaker's words. This technology is in some cases based on speech-recognition programs — that means the words on the screen are a transcription of how the words *sound*. The results are sometimes confusing and often amusing.

For example, a character suggested that another should take Aleve, the painkiller. The words on the screen were "take a leave" — meaning *get outta here already!* The on-screen version of "the ultimate in convenience" was "the ultimate inconvenience." I heard of another instance in which the speaker's words must have been "many accidents on the highway," because the words on the television screen were "maniacs see dents on the highway."

Such mistakes of the ear are often called *mondegreens*. That curious word was coined in the 1950s by author Sylvia Wright, who recalled how she once misunderstood a line from a Scottish ballad titled "The Bonny Earl O' Morey." She thought the line went: "They have slain the Earl Amurray/ and Lady Mondegreen." Her romantic notion was that the Earl and his true love, the Lady Mondegreen, died together heroically in the same cause.

Only much later did she discover that the ballad really said that after they killed the Earl, they *laid him on the green*.

The word "mondegreen" stuck.

Many mondegreens come from songs and recitations, and children specialize in them. One of the best known is "Gladly, the cross-eyed bear," from a hymn's "Gladly the cross I'd bear." For many of the young, "round yon virgin" will always be "round John Virgin." The national anthem's Jose is well known: *Jose, can you see*? Richard Stans is famous, too, among children who pledge allegiance: "and to the republic for Richard Stans." Children also salute Shirley Murphy in this version of the 23rd Psalm: "Shirley, good Mrs. Murphy, shall follow me all the days of my life."

The young sometimes cite a passage of the Lord's Prayer: "and lead us not into Penn Station," while others say: "and lead a snot into temptation." Some kids performing MacBeth see the witches' "double double toil and trouble" as "double double toilet trouble."

That mondegreens often make no sense seems to bother no one — although who could assail the logic of "through the night with a light from a *bulb*?"

William Safire's language column once took up the subject of big-name mondegreens. He mentioned that he once thought Guy Lombardo's name was Guylum Bardo, and his readers donated their own celebrity mondegreens: "Victor Moan" for Vic Damone, "Gorvey Doll" for Gore Vidal, "Big Spider Beck" for Bix Beiderbeck, "Sophie Aloran" for . . . you know.

I once wrote a column on mondegreens for *The Dallas Morning News*, and readers quickly responded with their own. One thought there was a famous woman singer named "Elephants Gerald." Another thought the "Londonderry Air" was the "London Derrière." Another wrote that when he was in high school, he thought a line in his school song was "we're loyal through the weedy parts," and found out only much later that the lyric was actually "we're loyal and true though we depart."

Misheard song lyrics show that we'll tolerate all kinds of bafflement in music. A reader said that he sang Patti Page's "leave your fickle past behind you" as "leave your pickle patch behind you." A second wrote that he thought for years that a line from "Groovin' on a Sunday Afternoon" — "you and me endlessly" — was "you and me and Leslie." He said he never could figure out how Leslie fit in, but that maybe it was some sort of ménage à trois.

A unique mondegreen was one reader's understanding of "The answer, my friend, is blowin' in the wind. The answer is blowin' in the wind." He thought those lines were "The ants are our friends. They're blowin' in the wind. The ant, sir, is blowin' in the wind." He said he thought it was some sort of environmental comment.

The best mondegreen in my own experience was created by a hotel clerk in 1989. She had taken a message from my secretary at *The Dallas Morning News,* who had called to say we'd won a Pulitzer Prize. But the slip of paper the clerk handed me seemed at first to have something to do with a chicken casserole. It read: "We want a pullet surprise."

CHAPTER 5

PRE- AND SUFFIXATION

A pivotal moment in Billy Wilder's 1960 film "The Apartment" has Jack Lemmon saying: "That's the way it crumbles . . . cookie-wise!"

As you might guess, the acerbic Wilder is poking fun at the "windfoggery" of office life. Lemmon plays a clerk in an insurance office who curries favor with the firm's execs in part by aping their language.

The movie's dialogue eagerly plays on the windfoggery theme. An exec says: "Premium-wise and billing-wise, we are 18 percent ahead of last year, October-wise." Lemmon says to another character: "As far as I'm concerned you're tops. I mean, decency-wise." And when she asks if she should light candles, he responds: "It's a must! Gracious living-wise."

Borrowing from the dialogue, the film's tagline announced: "Movie-wise, there has never been anything like it — laugh-wise, love-wise or otherwise-wise!"

That was funny and novel stuff a half century ago. But recently a TV news anchor said that "budget-wise and policy-wise preplanning" should be "finalized" soon. I half-expected him to conclude: And that's the way it crumbles . . . newswise.

What is this pervasive "prefixation" and "suffixation"

disease? We know it's epidemic when media writers pick it up — when a news anchor can read perfectly atrocious copy with a perfectly straight face.

"-Ize" and "-wise" are great offenders, as the examples above suggest. We've grown used to "Let's see what the picture is, weather-wise" instead of the sleeker "Let's see what the weather is." *Democratize, crystallize* and *theorize* are examples of nouns legitimately made verbs by adding the suffix "-ize." But a slain officer's being "funeralized" the next day? A reviewer who writes that a film is a "fictionized," rather than fictional, account? A reporter who is examining "certain contemporary themes, family-wise and religion-wise"?

Should we call those coinages "verbized" nouns?

Ungainly suffixes and prefixes detract from precision and polish. Happily, ugly words typically don't catch on if there's already a more attractive word for the job. Or even if they do catch on, they're still widely despised — the offensive *utilize* instead of *use*, for example, a pretentious reminder of our enchantment with unnecessary syllables.

It's true that prefixes and suffixes can create attractive and economical new words that strengthen expression. The suffix "-wise" makes legitimate and useful adverbs such as *lengthwise* or *crosswise*. Likewise, *likewise*.

But as professional writers and editors, we need to know the difference between the refined and the ridiculous.

Take the prefix "pre-." *Prejudice*, for example, comes from "pre" and "judge," a meaningful combination that defines the careless habit of closed minds — judging before knowing or considering the facts.

Prescient, too, is a word of unique intent, combining

roots that mean "fore" and "knowledge." And it's easy to see why *precaution* caught on: to take care beforehand. *Prehistory* is meaningful as well: What happened before we started recording it.

The flight attendant's "pre-board" seems to mean to get on the plane before you get on the plane. By the same token, how can one "pre-plan" or "pre-arrange" or "pre-establish"? You *must* plan and arrange and establish beforehand. A word such as "pre-plan" means something akin to planning to plan.

And that word "prequel." "Sequel," from a Latin root meaning "to follow," was sensible. Then along came "pre-quel," meaning preceding in action but following in presentation. Clever but freaky.

A builder "pre-sells" units in a housing project still under construction. Yes, I understand he'll use that money to finish the project, but what's going to happen after he's pre-sold and we've pre-purchased? Isn't he really just selling, and we just buying?

We're told we're "pre-approved" for credit cards or loans — for which we must still apply and be approved. So what does "pre-approved" mean? Maybe it means only: We have your name and address.

Is something so wrong with the concept of a used car that we must instead buy a "pre-owned" vehicle?

My husband once found an out-of-print book I'd wanted and bought it for me. Because it was used, he warned (or should I say "prewarned"?) that the book was "pre-read."

But he was *kidding*.

CHAPTER 6

SAM'S DICTIONARY

The updated version of *Webster's Ninth New Collegiate Dictionary* has 40 new words. That's no mean task, compiling the etymologies, definitions, pronunciations, and perhaps even usage examples for 40 new words.

But the mind turns irresistibly to the 17th century and to lexicographer Samuel Johnson, who wrote definitions not for 40 words, but for *40,000.* Johnson, you'll remember, was the author of what is considered the first comprehensive English dictionary. Not that there were no dictionaries before Dr. Johnson, but his work was the standard English dictionary until the 20th century's exhaustive Oxford English Dictionary.

Samuel Johnson undertook his monumental work not long after the French national dictionary was published — a task that took 40 French academicians 40 years to complete. Dr. Johnson did the same thing for the more voluminous English language in *nine* years, and he did it virtually alone, with only six clerks to help sort and compile.

Johnson's concern for correct pronunciation and usage prompted him to undertake the dictionary project. Since the early 1600s, there had been heavy criticism of the so-called corruption of the language. Writers and scholars were certain that English was being so badly debased that the days of its proper use were numbered.

Sound familiar?

In 1746, Johnson, in his mid-30s but already celebrated as a poet and critic, agreed to write the dictionary. He and his six clerks worked in a garret, stationing themselves at a long table that ran the room's length. That set-up allowed them to move about the table as they sorted and positioned their thousands of notes, lists, and other bits of paper.

They worked that way for nine years. Johnson not only wrote the definitions — he also collected more than 100,000 quotations as illustrations for the words' meanings — a practice adopted by the OED. And, remember, he had scant earlier work to build on, no research library, no shelves of reference works, no (horrors!) Internet.

Yet, when he published his *Dictionary of the English Language* in 1755, he had a work unrivalled in size and purpose for more than a hundred and fifty years.

The Johnson dictionary still doesn't have a rival in terms of originality and personality. We can't call all of Johnson's definitions completely unbiased. Some of them are famous, in fact, for both opinion and wit. For example, he defines "lexicographer" as "a writer of dictionaries, a harmless drudge." And the eternal competition among Great Britain's various peoples can be seen in Johnson's definition of "oats": "A grain, which in England is generally given to horses, but in Scotland supports the people."

Most scholars consider the Johnson dictionary a model of clarity, precision and economy of phrasing. And the achievement was even more impressive considering its author's unpromising beginnings.

Samuel Johnson was born in 1709 to an impoverished bookseller and emerged from his sickly infancy and childhood hard of hearing and blind in one eye. But his thirst for learning and the books in his father's shop gave him early and formidable knowledge. One of the great disappointments in Johnson's life was that he could not afford an education and had to leave Oxford after only a year, before earning a degree.

Nevertheless, he embarked in his mid-20s on a writing career of such prodigious output that he became known as a titan scholar and wordsmith. He also earned an honorary university degree and is identified even today as "Dr. Johnson." He's also recognized as the second most-quoted person in the English language, after Shakespeare.

Despite the volume and quality of his work, it never made him rich — although he did earn 1,575 pounds for his nine years of work on the dictionary. That was less than $3,000 dollars in today's money, yet it was a tidy sum in the 1700s and surely helped to ease the poverty that had dogged him all his life.

However much it was, though, how do you pay for what Samuel Johnson created — which is still called the cornerstone of the English language?

CHAPTER 7

THE CAMPAIGN
FOR PLAIN ENGLISH

The Plain English Campaign, a British group that pro-
motes clarity in writing, grants awards internationally for
the best and worst communications of the year. It attends
especially to "public information," and in addition to its
overall Plain English category, it focuses on government,
media and Web writing.

The group's "booby" prizes are in two categories: The
Golden Bull Awards and the Foot in Mouth Award — that
last for speech rather than writing.

Media writers can learn a lot from the Plain English
Campaign, which has more than 8,000 members in 80
countries. The group defines public information as "anything people have to read to get by in their daily lives,"
and plain English as "language that the intended audience can understand and act upon from a single reading."

Among the eight recipients of Golden Bulls last year
was the Bank of Scotland, for this opening on a letter to
consumers: "We hereby give you notice that Bank of
Scotland have retrocessed, reponed and restored
Executors and Assignees, in and to their own right and
place in the undernoted policy of Assurance by our Office,

Videlicet . . . ."

British Airways also received a Golden Bull Award, for the following paragraph, unreadable not only for its content but also for its all-cap form:

NOTE — CANCELLATIONS — BEFORE DEPARTURE FARE IS REFUNDABLE. IF COMBINING A NON-REFUNDABLE FARE WITH A REFUNDABLE FARE ONLY THE Y/C/J-CLASS HALF RETURN AMOUNT CAN BE REFUNDED. AFTER DEPARTURE FARE IS REFUNDABLE. IF COMBINING A NON-REFUNDABLE FARE WITH A REFUNDABLE FARE REFUND THE DIFFERENCE /IF ANY/BETWEEN THE FARE PAID AND THE APPLICABLE NORMAL BA ONEWAY FARE.

Among 2003's Golden Bull "winners" was jungle.com, for its response to a simple e-mailed query: "Do you still sell blank CDs?" The company replied:

We are currently in the process of consolidating our product range to ensure that the products that we stock are indicative of our brand aspirations. As part of our range consolidation we have also decided to revisit our supplier list and employ a more intelligent system for stock acquisition. As a result of the above certain product lines are now unavailable through jungle.com, whilst potentially remaining available from more mainstream suppliers.

The plain English answer to the question? No.

A 2003 Golden Bull also went to Marks and Spencer for a label on its chicken salad. The label, which said "Roast Chicken Salad," also wore a bright tag saying "Now With Roast Chicken!" The Plain English folks wondered nervously: "So what was in it before?"

Last year's Foot in Mouth Award went to British politician Boris Johnson for his statement: "I could not fail to disagree with you less."

Plain English awards often go to British concerns and personalities, but Brits don't have a monopoly on baffling commentary. Americans won the Foot in Mouth Award three of the four times it was granted from 2000 to 2003.

2003: U.S. Secretary of Defense Donald Rumsfeld for comments in a press briefing:

Reports that say that something hasn't happened are always interesting to me, because as we know, there are known knowns; there are things we know we know. We also know there are known unknowns; that is to say we know there are some things we do not know. But there are also unknown unknowns — the ones we don't know we don't know.

2002: Actor Richard Gere: "I know who I am. No one else knows who I am. If I was a giraffe and somebody said I was a snake, I'd think 'No, actually I am a giraffe.' "

2000: Hollywood star Alicia Silverstone: "I think that 'Clueless' was very deep. I think it was deep in the way that it was very light. I think lightness has to come from a very deep place if it's true lightness."

I think that we could all agree that those Golden Bull and Foot in Mouth winners deserve their distinction. But if pretensions and gobbledygook earn a booby prize, what do the Plain English folk consider truly winning writing?

They like short sentences, simple vocabulary, active verbs, personal pronouns such as "you" and "we," and a clear, natural, human, conversational, meaningful style.

Sounds good to me.

CHAPTER 8

PREFERRED PRONUNCIATIONS

A dinner party guest described someone as wearing a dour expression, pronouncing it "DOWer," and another guest said that *dour* was correctly pronounced "DOOer." Disagreement went around the table. To settle the question, the host produced his dictionary, thumbed to the D's and announced — to some surprise — that "DOOer" was the preferred pronunciation.

Nobody asked the host if he had other dictionaries. But later some of us consulted other volumes and came up with the preferred pronunciation of "DOWer." So I rounded up all the usual dictionaries and grilled them. Turns out that the preferred pronunciation of *dour* is in dispute, at least in the United States. The British apparently widely accept the "DOOer" pronunciation. But even in the United States, the dinner host's dictionary ruled on the side of the majority: Most American dictionaries also prefer "DOOer."

This anecdote points out an interesting but neglected fact about dictionaries: There are many, and they sometimes disagree. Yet we refer to "the dictionary," as though there were only one and it were Holy Writ. But dictionaries (so called because they reflect *diction*) are created by committees — and committees can come up with different conclusions. We haven't depended upon a single dictionary since lone lexicographer Samuel Johnson created his comprehensive English dictionary in the 1700s.

Besides, the language is constantly evolving. As we've supposed since Heraclitus explored the idea of constant flux five or six hundred years before Christ, *things change.* And what we find when we dip our toes into the stream of change may depend upon exactly where we stand on the bank.

Neither change nor disagreement means that we're operating in linguistic chaos, however. Change is slow and disagreement healthy, and there are enough "rules" to satisfy the most demanding language purist.

Saying things the *right* way matters to all of us, of course. But it's of special concern to those in television and radio because how they say things can make them more or less credible to their listeners. A television anchor recently pronounced *Caribbean* differently each time he said it — sometimes with the emphasis on RIB and sometimes with it on BEE. (Most dictionaries prefer CariBEEan.) A radio newscaster pronounced *envelope* alternately in the same sentence as ENvelope and ONvelope. (ENvelope is preferred.) Still another newscaster repeatedly said "renumerate" instead of *remunerate.*

We're seldom near a dictionary when we're troubled about how to say a word. And when we're near a dictionary, we can't remember the words we meant to look up. And when pronunciations are in transition or dispute, we'd need to consult not one but a *handful* of dictionaries.

Below is a modest compendium of frequently mispronounced words. These pronunciations represent the consensus of commonly used dictionaries — *Webster's New World, Webster's College, American Heritage,* and *Random House College.*

We don't even need a dictionary to discuss some of the most annoying mispronunciations. Like the newscaster who said "renumerate," we have only to *look* at the words. Three examples are "nucular" instead of NUclear, "realator" instead of REALtor and "athalete" instead of ATHlete. The problem is the same in each case: The speakers are pronouncing syllables that *aren't there.*

Mischievous also frequently suffers a syllable it doesn't possess. Instead of MISchievous, some say "misCHEEVeeous." *Heinous, grievous,* and *intravenous* are likewise words that can contain unwelcome syllables — making them "HAYneeous," "GREEveeous" and "intraVAYneeous."

Jewelry is *jewel* with "ree" added, but it's frequently mispronounced "JUleree." *Irrelevant* is mispronounced by transposing letters — so that the word becomes "irREVelant." *Liaison* should be pronounced with a stressed and long A in the middle: "lee-A-zahn." But for some reason, people create new first and second syllables and say it "LAY-uh-zon."

The same kind of word myopia exists for "ekcetera" instead of *etcetera*, "asterik" instead of *asterisk*, and "axe" instead of *ask*.

A common mispronunciation arises through misunderstanding: saying "fortAY" instead of "fort" when we mean the French *forte*. Some speakers confuse the French *forte*, pronounced "fort" and meaning strong point, with the

Italian *forte,* pronounced "fortAY" and meaning loud or loudly.

Mispronouncing *Italian, Iraq,* and *Iran as* EYEtalian, EYEraq, and EYEran is a teeth-gritter. That beginning I is short and sounds like the I in *it.*

The non-word *irregardless* makes many fume — not because of *how* it's said, but that it's said at all. The syllables "ir" and "less" create a double negative, so *regardless* suffices.

The word *extraordinary* is "exTRORDinary," not "extra-ordinary." *Interesting* is "INtristing," not "inneresting." The H on *herb* is silent: "erb." *Flaccid* is "FLAXid," not "flassid." It's IMpotent, not "imPOtent," *height* and not "heighth." *Bade* and *forbade* are "bad," not "bayed." The preferred pronunciation of *accessory* is "akSESSry," not "aSSESSry."

Pronunciation in English is tricky and hard to remember. It may be some comfort to paraphrase William Safire: In matters of pronunciation and usage, when enough of us are wrong, we're right.

CHAPTER 9

A ROAST BY ANY OTHER NAME

A friend once called me after a dinner party at my house.

"What was that wonderful dish you served as an appetizer last night, and could I have the recipe?"

"Calamari," I said. And when I realized she was drawing a blank, I added, "Squid."

Short silence. We chatted a few minutes more, and she did not renew her request for the recipe.

What we call things matters — especially if we're going to eat them. Calamari? Yum. Squid? Well, that's another kettle of seafood.

In "Giant," a 1956 film starring Elizabeth Taylor and Rock Hudson, the three small children of the Hudson/Taylor characters help fatten up a turkey they come to know as Pedro. Come Thanksgiving Day, a golden roast bird is brought to the table amid *oohs* and *ahs*. The children's faces are alight — until someone lets slip the name "Pedro." "Pedro?" they ask one by one, smiles fading and horror dawning. Shortly, all three children are sobbing inconsolably.

Of course, they eat nothing. It was OK to eat turkey, but it was not OK — not OK at all — to eat *Pedro*.

Personalizing that bird with a human name made it inedible. Fowl and fish generally retain their labels when we eat them — roast turkey sounds delicious, as does pheasant under glass or sole au gratin. But roast Pedro? No.

Four-legged food is another matter. We generally rename those animals to make them seem less mammal and more edible. We have no recipes for cow under glass or hog au gratin. We don't like to think of tucking into a hunk of cow, calf, hog, sheep, deer, or goat — instead, we eat beef, veal, pork, mutton, venison, cabrito. And the better acquainted we are with the type of animal on the plate, the more apt we are to give it an alias before we eat it. (Lamb is a notable exception.) Squeamishness is quelled as well because four-legged food seldom resembles itself on the plate. Fish and fowl can look much the same — minus feather and scale. But a hunk of meat resembles only a hunk of meat.

The critical point is what we see in our mind's eye when we hear a word. Why would we rather eat escargot than snails? Because escargot calls to mind a piping hot, fragrant, buttery treat; snails hump along the earth in a trail of slime. I've eaten plenty of escargot, but — in my mind, at least — never a snail.

I've also eaten bear and buffalo and, for me, both made distressing dining. Bear was the worst — without an alias, it was undeniably . . . *bear*. Which bear? Mama? Papa? Baby Bear? Bruno? It might have been delicious, but I don't remember how it tasted. Maybe if it had been called something else, something from another language — casserole d'ours (délicieux!) or de oso (delicioso!) or der bär (köstlich!). But as it was, it wouldn't have taken much for me to screw up my face and — shades of Roast Pedro — sob.

Irrational? No. In cuisine, as in all things, words matter.

CHAPTER 10

OK, OK

Allen Walker Read, word sleuth, died October 16. If that name doesn't ring a bell, here's something that will: *OK*.

Whether we spell it *OK, O.K.,* or *okay*, that little word is unquestionably the world's best-known Americanism. It has been incorporated into languages all over the globe and is used and understood by people who may not know another word of English. H.L. Mencken called the word "the most shining and successful Americanism ever invented."

But *OK*'s origin was a mystery until the early 1940s, when Allen Read revealed its derivation. Dr. Read, who was 96 when he died and who spent his long professional life unraveling linguistic mysteries, was known as the "OK expert." That was hardly his only triumph, just his most famous. And it was no mean feat, considering the many controversial theories advanced regarding *OK*'s origin before Dr. Read did his definitive detective work.

Even cursory research yields a handful of suggestions for how *OK* came to be. One credible notion was that the word was adapted from the Choctow Indian word *okeh*, meaning "it is so and is no other way." Another interesting theory was that crates of fine Haitian rum and molasses from Aux Cayes (pronounced ohKAY) carried the port of shipment's phonetic notation, "OK." A more fanciful speculation was that the word came from a superior U.S. Army biscuit called OK biscuits.

The "OK" speculation ended, writes lexicographer Wilfred Funk, when Allen Read published his research in a 1941 issue of *Saturday Review of Literature*. In that article, Dr. Read explained that *OK* was an abbreviation for a deliberate misspelling of "all correct" — that is, "oll korrect." A journalism fad in the 1830s was using humorous abbreviations — for example, S.P. for "small potatoes" or R.T.B.S. for "remains to be seen." The abbreviation "O.K." first appeared in its current sense in 1839 in *The Boston Morning Post*.

While other newspaper abbreviations died away, "OK" stuck. Why? Because it was used in a presidential election campaign. In 1840 President Martin Van Buren was up for re-election. Van Buren, born in Kinderhook, N.Y., was also known as "Old Kinderhook." His partisans took the letters O and K from "Old Kinderhook," calling themselves the "OK Club" and adopting "OK" as their slogan — thus both borrowing and fortifying OK's meaning of "all right!"

And a word was born — a little word that became America's leading linguistic export.

Allen Read did much more than investigate the word *OK*. He tracked down the origins of many words. He once hitchhiked to Iowa from Missouri to check out the birth of the word "blizzard." He contributed to Funk & Wagnall's, Random House, and other dictionaries. He was an editor of the Dictionary of American English. He wrote entries for the Encyclopaedia Britannica. He was professor of English at Columbia University for nearly 30 years. H.L. Mencken said that Dr. Read knew more about early Americanisms "than anyone else on earth."

So we can probably understand why he was less than thrilled that his work on other words and expressions was eclipsed by his work on *OK*. Still, that little word was among the first few uttered on the moon. Everyone remembers "Houston, Tranquility Base here; the Eagle has landed," but those weren't the first words spoken after the landing. In fact, Buzz Aldrin spoke first, with a status report that began: "Contact light: OK . . . ."

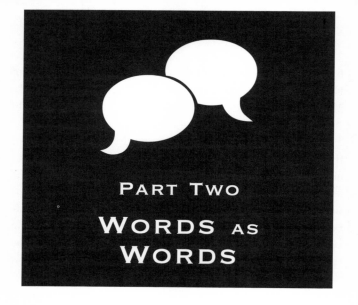

PART TWO

WORDS AS WORDS

CHAPTER 11

LOST WORDS

I recently saw the word "spondulicks," old-time slang for money, spelled "spondulix" in a newspaper column. Curious, I consulted several desk dictionaries to check the word's spelling and was surprised to find it wasn't listed at all. Sure, it's an antique word, maybe even moribund. But dead and gone? From the dictionary untimely ripped, to paraphrase Shakespeare?

Like all living things, the language is in constant flux, changing slightly over time, gaining new words and losing old. At 600,000 recorded words and counting, English has a huge lexicon — hundreds of thousands more than any other language. As that lexicon grows, some words are forgotten, unused, or unnecessary, and dictionaries drop them to make room for newer words. Such words are usually housed elsewhere, though — in the many volumes of the Oxford English Dictionary, say, or in a collection of ancient words such as Susan Sperling's *Poplollies and Bellibones: A Celebration of Lost Words.*

In any case, it's easier to discover a word's birthday than its obituary. In a foreword to Susan Sperling's collection, wordsmith Willard Espy writes that it's best to consider "dead" words merely missing or presumed dead: "Even after being embalmed by linguists and formally laid out in their coffins for interment, words have a way of sitting up, calling for a sip of water to restore their strength and returning as lively as ten-year-old children to their verbal rounds."

Poplollies and Bellibones lists many of the "presumed dead." *Thrip, brangle, murfle*, and *paggle* once led perfectly respectable lives, for example, and it would be nice if they were resurrected. *Thrip* was especially useful — it meant to snap one's fingers. The expressive *brangle* named what we now less colorfully call an argument. *Murfle?* A pimple or a zit. *Paggle* meant to bulge or hang loosely. Have a murfle and a paggle just sounds like more *fun* than having a pimple and a potgut.

Too bad we lost *snertle*, meaning to snicker. Or *brool*, a low, deep murmuring. *Blutter* was a good word for blurting something out. A *hufty-tufty* was a boorish braggart. *Sloomy* was how we felt when we were lazy and drowsy. *Pash* was a nice emphatic word for forehead. *Ribble* meant wrinkle or furrow — as in ribbling your pash.

Some antique words make so much sense that it's a wonder we lost them. One such is *downsteepy*, meaning precipitous or steep. *Fellowfeeling* was an expressive word for empathy. *Turngiddy* meant dizzy, and *kew-kaw* meant upside down. *Wink-a-peeps* were eyes. *Flesh-spades* were fingernails. *Chinkers* were coins. *Kill-priest* was port wine.

We could still use *blob-tale*, a gossip. Same goes for the *crush-room*, a theater hall or lobby where the audience goes between acts. A *fearbabe* was something designed to scare the baby. *Chair day* was a gentle idiom for old age — that time of life spent largely in rest and inactivity.

Do we have so many words for infidelity that we no longer have room for the evocative *bedswerver* or *spouse-break*?

Have we a modern substitute for *smellsmock*, an errant clergyman?

Where's our common word for feeling happy and sad at the same time? One considers *nostalgic, poignant, sentimental, melancholy,* but they fall short. *Bittersweet* comes close, but once we had *merry-go-sorry* — or *chantpleure*, which means to sing and weep at the same time.

Some antique words are notably onomatopoetic (making the sound they name). One of the definitions for *tittup*, for example, is the sound of a horse's hooves as it canters or prances. *Rooped* and *roaky*, pertaining to the voice, meant hoarse or thick. *Quop* meant to throb, as in "My heart began to *quop!*"

Some lost words should stay lost, however. What we call junk food, ugly enough in its own right, once was called *lubber-wort. Belly-timber* was food, and to *glop* was to swallow greedily. A *muckender* was a bib. A kiss was the unromantic *lipclap*. Pleasure was far less pleasant when it was *adlubescence*. And I guess we can do without *snotter-clout*, a handkerchief, or *sparrow-fart,* which meant daybreak. The cosmetic we call eyeshadow once was *calliblephary* (accent on *bleph*), and rouge or blusher was called *fucus*.

No, I'm not making this up.

Back to that old word *spondulicks*: I found it. It was at rest in the commodious Oxford English Dictionary, with a metaphorical robe over its knees. Its chair day, presumably. "Aha!" I bluttered in adlubescence when I cast my wink-a-peeps on it, slapping my pash and thripping. "There you are!"

I could have chantpleured.

CHAPTER 12

NEW WORDS:
LANGUAGE MIRRORS SOCIETY

One of the benefits of a sprawling, vibrant, receptive language such as English is its willingness — even eagerness — to embrace new words and expressions. With its lexicon of more than 600,000 words, English is by far the largest language in history, and its growth shows no sign of abating.

New words can come from everywhere and everything — from any discipline, specialty, or activity. Whatever the source of new words, their course through the language is hastened by the mass media in general and by media writers in particular.

The media not only help spread new language from all quarters, they also produce it when they coin terms to describe themselves and their activities. Media-related words are especially interesting because they often have social "resonance." They're not just appropriate or imaginative describers of a certain medium, but they also say something important about our larger world. The hybrid "infotainment," for example, merges information and entertainment, just as some media increasingly do. The hybrid word not only reflects that fact, but it also tells us something about our society and our society's values, pressures, and trends.

Infotainment has been around for a long time, but *zitcom*, a television show that features or appeals to teenagers, is more recent. *Zitcom* is a play on *sitcom*, or situation comedy, and it of course alludes to acne, the adolescent's bane. The very existence of a word such as *zitcom* suggests how important appealing to the young is to the entertainment world and to Madison Avenue. That importance derives from money — specifically, youth's spending power. But that we even have or need such a word also suggests American society's general preoccupation with youth as well as its indulgence of the young. In many cultures, young people are "kept in their place," a place that offers neither money nor power.

Another revealing hybrid is *irritainment*, which refers to media events or shows that are at once annoying and compelling. Television's Jerry Springer springs to mind, but there's no shortage of abhorrent material on television — a medium that was once the subject of a new term now grown old: *vast wasteland*. Television has no monopoly on irritainment, though. Most material worthy of the name is shallow, without intellectual content, and debases rather than elevates humankind. The movie "Dumb & Dumber," in correctly naming itself, showed another aspect of *irritainment* — not only is it unashamed of its own baseness, it seems oddly proud of it. That response mirrors the defiantly lowered standards of certain segments of society in which being dumb — or even dumber — is a badge of honor. We hear of certain students being ostracized by their peers, for example, because they study and care about their grades.

Another new hybrid is *shockumentary*, a reality program showing actual violence or accidents. The "can't look away" popularity of reality shows suggests both our national fascination with, and anxiety about, violence. *Adrenaline TV* also refers to the telecasting of frightening or horrifying real events.

A blend of *carnage* and *pornography* gives us *carnography*, which refers to extended scenes of violence. The word has been used to describe, for example, the long and graphic battle scenes in "Saving Private Ryan" and "Blackhawk Down."

Although *carnography* uses *pornography's* suffix, a handful of new words borrow that word's prefix to identify anything excessive, garish, phony, or empty. "Porn" words abound. *Eco-porn*, for example, refers to advertisements that laud the policies of companies known for gross environmental pollution.

A curiosity from the '90s is *domestic porn* — books, movies and TV that present artificial and idealized images of the perfect home, family and home life. Those images abounded in the '50s, and not many scoffed. No more. The reaction to domestic porn probably accounts for the otherwise puzzling but widespread animosity toward Domestic Goddess Martha Stewart well before her stock-selling scandal.

Investment porn and *financial porn* are related coinages that refer to articles profiling and glorifying financiers, money managers, and notable financial success in general. Best-seller lists nearly always include books that pay homage to the rich and to riches. Investment porn and financial porn content is nothing new — only its labels are. And the new terms suggest a certain canniness in our ability to look at ourselves analytically if not critically.

The converse of investment and financial porn is *debt porn* — stories profiling people whose massive debt brings them down. *Debt porn* pieces usually rely on the confessional first person: *I was a Credit Card Junkie; Red Ink Ruined My Life; Debt Cost Me My Home and Family.* Debt porn is the credit-card version of confessionals like the movie "Days of Wine and Roses" — or even earlier, "The Lost Weekend." Both were film stories of alcoholism, old-hat now that we have so many other addictions.

New expressions are interesting as words, but they're also interesting as mirrors: They reflect what a society honors and despises, or hopes and fears.

CHAPTER 13

PLACE AS METAPHOR

The Vatican, according to news reports, may abolish the concept of Limbo — which for seven centuries has named a netherworld place for the dead who don't qualify for Heaven but don't deserve Hell.

It's one thing to abolish a place — especially if it's also decreed that the place never existed — and another to abolish a *concept*. How do you vanquish a metaphor? Whatever Pope Benedict XVI decides, we'll still say we're in Limbo when we mean we're in a state of suspension — neither here nor there.

Language is rich in place as metaphor — whether it exists in fact or is just a state of mind. If we're not in Limbo, we might be in Shangri-La or Siberia. We might meet our Waterloo, visit the Slough of Despond, or cross the Rubicon. Maybe we can stop on the road to Damascus and eventually even slouch toward Bethlehem.

We can do all that, and everyone understands we haven't been anywhere, except in spirit.

Place metaphors are widely understood even if we don't know their origins. We may not know that Limbo derives from the Latin *limbus,* which means "hem" or "edge," but we know what it means in common parlance. We know that Siberia, which seems to be Hell's climatic opposite, also seems to be about as much fun. Ditto the "Slough of Despond," a term from John Bunyan's *Pilgrim's Progress* meaning deep depression. A slough is a quagmire, a bog in which one becomes stuck, and Despond, as you would guess, comes from the same root as *despondent*.

Hell is the ultimate metaphor for a bad trip. We know that the Hades of Greek myth and Milton's Pandemonium — Hell's capital in Paradise Lost — are just alternate routes to the same awful destination.

Not so Shangri-La, from James Hilton's 1933 novel, *Lost Horizons*. That paradise of peace and eternal youth moved into everyday use with a 1937 movie starring Ronald Colman, and, later, with a popular song that included the lyric "Your kisses take me to Shangri-La."

There's no shortage of metaphor for the idealized place. Heaven awaits, and so does its Nordic equivalent, Valhalla. Sir Thomas More created Utopia in the 1500s, and we use that noun or the adjective *utopian* when we want to describe social and political perfection. The Greeks gave us Elysium, the Elysian Fields, and Arcadia. Samuel Coleridge, in opium-induced delirium, dreamed up the fantastic Xanadu, a luxurious pleasure palace.

Place also makes great metaphors for transition or transformation. The New Testament's "Road to Damascus" is an example. Scripture says that the rabbi Saul of Tarsus was on that road when he saw a great light, heard Jesus speak, was immediately converted to Christianity, and thereafter became Paul the Apostle. We speak of our "Road to Damascus" to refer to a personal moment of revelation or transformation.

"Crossing the Rubicon" is another transition term. It

refers to a decisive point of action — a river of no return. The expression comes from 49 B.C., when Julius Caesar's army crossed the Rubicon, a river dividing Italy from Gaul. The Roman Senate knew that crossing the small river would mean war and had forbidden Caesar to do so. But he stepped into the water anyway, supposedly uttering: "The die is cast."

Meeting our "Waterloo" is also a moment of transition — one that means defeat. Waterloo, a village near Brussels, was the scene of Napoleon's downfall.

Yet another celebrated term of transition is "Slouching toward Bethlehem" — usually interpreted to mean the birth of a chaotic and unknown future. The expression is from William Butler Yeats' "Second Coming," which asks "what great beast, its hour come round at last, slouches towards Bethlehem to be born?" Writer Joan Didion used the term to title a famous late-60s essay, and humorist Peter De Vries less somberly spoofed the famous expression when he titled one of his novels *Slouching Towards Kalamazoo*.

There's no end of metaphorical places to go. The best part — or the worst, depending upon the destination — is that we all have a ticket to ride.

CHAPTER 14

PLAYING FOOTSIE

A columnist wrote that George W. Bush had once again "put his foot in it," when the columnist actually meant "put his foot in his mouth."

It makes a difference — the two expressions don't mean the same thing.

You put your foot in your mouth when you say something embarrassing or awkward — it's a *verbal* faux pas. A friend put her foot in her mouth, for example, when she asked a fat woman who was not pregnant when her baby was due.

Putting your foot in it, however, means stepping in something foul. It's a metaphorical misstep — the opposite of "putting your foot right" — and one that has unfortunate consequences. A thief, for example, made some purchases in a convenience store, then pulled a gun, held up the place, and sped away with his loot. How did he put his foot in it? He'd paid for his purchases with his credit card.

"Foot" expressions are common in both literal and figurative language and are usually clear from the context. We put our best foot forward or get our foot in the door. We're light on our feet, land on our feet, and think well on our feet. We're trying to get a foothold, or to get on equal footing. We'd like to leave our footprints in the sands of time.

When we've had enough, we put our foot down. Those with itchy feet are lucky if they're also footloose and fancy-free and don't end up with a driver who has a lead foot. We could end up where, as a student once wrote, "the hand of man has never set foot."

Or we don't want to go, so we drag our feet.

Show us some footlights, and we dazzle 'em with our footwork, bringing the crowd to its feet. The audience members, thus swept off their feet, will be at *our* feet. We might consider them lackeys, or footboys. They might even be sycophants — footkissers, footlickers, or bootlickers. They might wait on us hand and foot and remain underfoot — until they discover we have feet of clay. Then they will dash away, fleet of foot.

We call a newcomer or novice a tenderfoot, a frontier term for the dude whose feet are sore from new cowboy boots. We term an amateur or someone who lacks judgment or ability a footling. An insubstantial or inept person is footless, meaning, metaphorically, that he has no feet — thus, lacks foundation.

We might say of a judgmental person who wants everyone to conform to his standards: "He measures everyone's foot by his own last." (A *last* is a foot-shaped form used in shoemaking.)

We might say something is "footy" when we mean paltry or poor. The sound of a step is a footfall. We foot the bill. Or maybe we *don't* foot the bill and try to sneak away, like a slyboots or footpad. But we may be caught flat-footed — maybe by a flatfoot! Or by a gumshoe.

Slyboots and *footpad* (which means a petty thief, one who steals on foot) are interesting in that both French and German have similar expressions: *pied plat* (flat foot) and *leisenstreter* (light treader), each meaning one who moves stealthily and for clandestine purpose. Unlike the *pied plat* of French, however, the flatfoot of American English means a police officer and refers not to stealth, but rather to the fallen arches of one who walks a beat.

The Latin and Greek roots for the word *foot* are *ped* and *pod*. We see those prefixes in *podiatrist, pedal, pedestrian, pedicure, pedometer,* etc. We also see "pod" suffixes in words such as *arthropod* (certain invertebrate animals such as insects, arachnids, and crustaceans) or *pleopod,* meaning resembling a foot.

And, notably, we see the "foot" root in *podium,* which helps us remember that a podium is the platform a speaker stands *on*. The stand a speaker stands *at* and which holds notes and maybe a microphone is better called a *lectern* (related to *lecture*).

But that's just a footnote.

CHAPTER 15

WORDS FROM THE GODS

Here's nice alliteration, but poor metaphor: "His talent is untying the Gordian knots typical in tangled legal procedures." The reason it's poor metaphor is that the point of the Gordian knot myth was that it could *not* be untied. Rather, it was cut.

That is just one of many mythological expressions that can deepen and enrich our communication — provided we use them correctly.

"Cutting the Gordian knot" brings to mind an amusing scene in one of Harrison Ford's "Indiana Jones" films. In that scene, Indiana is confronted by a swordsman who elaborately, menacingly, and at length brandishes his blade. Indiana watches the swordsman's threatening histrionics for a few seconds, then offhandedly draws his pistol and shoots him.

It's just that sort of dispatch that Alexander the Great brought to the task of the Gordian knot. The expression comes from an ancient Greek tale in which King Gordius secures his chariot with a knot so complicated that a prophecy arises: Whoever can undo the knot will rule Asia. Eventually, Alexander encounters the Gordian knot and — with Indiana Jones nonchalance — simply draws his sword and cuts it.

Another well known mythological expression is "Achilles' heel," which we use to refer to a weak spot. "Achilles' heel" is an expression drawn from the legend that the mother of the infant Achilles dipped him into the magical river Styx to make him invulnerable. She held him by the heel, however, leaving it unprotected — and the heroic Achilles was killed in adulthood by an arrow to his heel. (Achilles also names the tendon at the back of the heel as well as the "Achilles reflex," an ankle jerk caused by tapping that tendon.)

Two other useful expressions from myth are "Herculean task," understood to be tough labor, and "Augean stables." Hercules, a demigod, was son of the Greek god Zeus and a mortal woman. The story goes that Hera, Zeus' wife, was so jealous of Hercules that she sent him a dozen impossible tasks — which he nevertheless accomplished, thereby becoming immortal.

One of Hercules' tasks was cleaning King Augeas' stables — which housed 3,000 oxen and hadn't been cleaned in 30 years. Hercules diverted two rivers through the stables and voilà! Today, we liken any awesome cleanup — often one involving massive corruption — to "cleaning the Augean stables."

The myths of mortals Pandora and Cassandra also provide useful allusions. In the mythic world, Pandora's curiosity was the source of all misfortune. The gods gave her a box into which each had put something harmful, forbidding her ever to open it. In time, her curiosity got the better of her, and she lifted the lid. Out flew all evil. References to "Pandora's Box" are common — for example, this play-on-words headline about lawyer advertising:

"Lawyers open Pandora's briefcase."

The mortal Cassandra's mistake was spurning the god Apollo's advances. He cursed her with a "gift" of prophecy: She would predict the future accurately, but her curse would be that no one would believe her. The Cassandra myth is frequently alluded to in modern life. For example, Warren Buffet — who repeatedly has warned accurately against various stock market euphorias — has been called a "Wall Street Cassandra."

From Eros, the Greek god of love, we get the word *erotic*, while from his counterpart, Aphrodite, comes *aphrodisiac* — something that excites sexual desire. Cupid and Venus, the Roman god and goddess of love, are not so complimented, however. From Cupid comes *cupidity*, which means an intense desire to possess, or avarice and greed, while from Venus comes *venereal* — as in venereal disease.

From Mars, the Roman god of war, comes *martial*. From Odysseus' friend Mentor, who was entrusted with the education of Odysseus' son, comes our noun *mentor*. From the Titans, called the elder gods, comes *titanic*. From Sisyphus' eternal task of rolling a large stone up a hill, only to see it roll down again, comes *Sisyphean*, an adjective we give to constant and thankless effort. From Nemesis, the Greek goddess of justice, comes our noun *nemesis*, which means a bane or a relentless opponent who seeks retribution. From Hector, a heroic figure in the Trojan army, comes the verb *hector*, meaning to tease, bully or badger.

Dionysian and *bacchanalian* are adjectives that describe wild and drunken celebration and derive from the Greek and Roman gods of revelry and wine, Dionysus and Bacchus.

Junoesque comes from Juno, wife of Jupiter (or Jove), the Roman equivalent of Zeus. *Junoesque* once suggested a stately, matronly beauty but is now commonly a euphemism for "queen-sized" — or, as I once heard it stated both inelegantly and redundantly, a "Junoesque fatso."

Jovial, meantime, derives from Jove — although he seemed far from jovial when he was lobbing thunderbolts at Earthlings. Maybe he had his lighter moments.

These and other allusions are the common property of the literate, and they reinforce and amplify a writer's or speaker's meanings. But they must be accurate, natural rather than contrived, and derived from a habit of wide reading.

CHAPTER 16

WORDS FOR THE FEARFUL

The horror genre has a concept that seems far more laughable than scary — the concept of the "Invisible Man." I mean: an empty suit — how scary is that? Yet terrified folks flee, shrieking: *Aiieee! There's nothing there!*

Literally, running from nothing.

Only those afraid of everything would run from nothing, if you follow me. And there is in fact such a fear — *pantophobia*, which means fear of everything. Fear of nothing — unless it's the kind of "nothing" presented by the Invisible Man — also has a name. It's *hypophobia*, or lack of fear.

Fear of everything and fear of nothing are equally irrational. And there's a big difference, of course, between fear and phobia. But judging from the huge number of "phobia" words, there's much to fear. A few better known terrors are *claustrophobia, agoraphobia, ochlophobia, ophidiophobia, musophobia,* and *brontophobia* — more commonly known as fear of closed spaces, open spaces, crowds, snakes, mice, and thunder.

Certain fears are so prevalent that popular culture capitalizes on them. Steven Spielberg's 1990 film "Arachnophobia" took fear of spiders to a comic extreme, for example. Acrophobia, or fear of heights, was a central theme in Alfred Hitchcock's 1958 movie "Vertigo." Fear of heights also afflicted British TV's beloved Inspector Morse. Aviatophobia lent novelist Erica Jong the richly symbolic title of her 1973 book, *Fear of Flying*.

The Oxford English Dictionary lists many odd, even outlandish phobia words. Such words also can be found in the *Insomniac's Dictionary of the Outrageous, Odd, and Unusual* by Paul Hellweg; *Crazy English*, by Richard Lederer; and *Words at Play* by O. V. Michaelsen.

For some, apparently, hell really *is* other people. *Anthropophobia* is fear of people, *androphobia* is fear of men, and *gynephobia*, fear of women. There's also *pediophobia*, fear of children; *parthenophobia*, fear of young girls; and *xenophobia*, fear of strangers or foreigners.

But do we really need a word such as *armenophobia*? Is fear of Armenians a viable category?

Some fears are understandable even if you don't share them — *dentophobia*, for example, fear of going to the dentist. We're not surprised that there's such a thing as *agrizoophobia* (fear of wild animals), *algophobia* (pain), *poinephobia* (punishment), *pyrophobia* (fire), and *hematophobia* (blood).

Thanatophobia, or fear of death, is a biggie, but another common phobia is *topophobia*, extreme stage fright or fear of performing in public. Studies have shown, in fact, that some people would rather face death than an audience.

One can understand *policophobia* (fear of the police) in certain circumstances. But *blennophobia*, *alliumphobia*, and *arachibutyrophobia*? Those phobias are fear of slime, of garlic, of getting peanut butter stuck to the roof of the mouth.

There's no shortage of curious phobias. *Triskaideka-phobia*, fear of the number 13, is well known. I was surprised to find we need such a word as *porphyrophobia* — fear of the color purple — until I discovered *chromophobia*, fear of color in general. There's a word for the malady afflicting those who can't stand prosperity — *chrematophobia*, or fear of money. And for those who are terrified of good news, there's *euphobia*.

One can readily imagine being fearful of the "midnight hours," as Wilson Pickett famously sang, but *eosophobia*? That's fear of dawn. Or how about *anthophobia*, fear of flowers? Extend that phobia a little and you have *botanophobia*, fear of both plants and flowers.

One group of phobias makes you wonder if folks have been reading too much *DaVinci Code*. *Paterophobia*, for example — fear of the Fathers of the early Church. *Ecclesiophobia* means fear of church; *hagiophobia*, fear of holy things; and *homilophobia*, fear of sermons.

Practice those phobias long enough, and another could be in the works: *hadephobia*, or fear of hell.

Could Franklin D. Roosevelt have had *phobophobia* in mind when he said, "The only thing we have to fear is fear itself"? *Phobophobia* is fear of fearing.

The world of politics has become so harrowing that one can imagine phobias springing up all over the place: *levophobia*: fear of things on the left, or *dextrophobia*, fear of things on the right. There's *misocainea*, fear of anything new, and *tropophobia*, fear of making changes. The phobia most likely to see some increase is *politicophobia*, or fear of politicians.

Even wordsmiths have fears. *Metrophobia*, for example, is fear of poetry. And don't mention "Madam I'm Adam" to sufferers of *aibohphobia*, fear of palindromes. (A palindrome is something that reads the same backward as forward. Notice that this cleverly named phobia — *aibohphobia* — is itself a palindrome).

There's even *phobologophobia* — a malady that could make reading this column a nightmare. It means a fear of phobia words.

CHAPTER 17

RUNNING WILD

Some of the smallest words in English shoulder the heaviest burden of meaning. The little word *run*, for example, occupies 15 pages in the Oxford English Dictionary — a little word, but hardly simple, whether a run in your stocking or a run-up in your stock.

Run has many meanings, but a basic one, both literally and figuratively, is motion, flowing or tending toward. The river ran over its banks. Her eyes ran over the page. His interest runs to medicine. A running stitch, a runny nose.

We hear a lot of "run" expressions in politics. Candidates are running. They may be giving opponents a good run for their money. They're in or out of the running. They select running mates. It might be a runaway election, or end in a runoff. And someone will be a runner-up.

Not surprisingly, such references come from the racing world. A "good run for your money" applies to a horse on which one has bet and which runs well, though without winning. "Running mate" was first used in the 1860s to refer to a horse that set the pace for another horse from the same stable. By 1890, "running mate" also had become a political term.

"Run" phrases are so common that you can produce

one by adding almost any preposition to the verb run. We run into or run across someone or something when we see someone or something by chance. We tell people to run along when we want them to scat. Run-in can refer to a quarrel or to printed matter inserted into a text. Poor writers create run-on sentences, and poor speakers run on and on.

A poorly maintained house is a run-down house, and a poorly maintained car may run down. When we want a summary or outline, we ask for a rundown, and if we don't get it, we say we got the runaround.

We run out of dough when we run through our inheritance and start running up debt. Our cup isn't running over.

We're on the run when hurrying or running away.

When we run off, it means something entirely different from the runoff after an election, or from the runoff after a storm. And if we run off with something or someone, we may be, as with errant lovers, running around. Maybe we've run out on someone. Maybe we're runaways who are running for it, and maybe someone will run after us, maybe run us to ground, or run us down, or even run over us. Serves us right.

We run something to ground when we find it. Run to ground or run to earth are fox-hunting metaphors that mean the prey has been chased to its burrow or hiding-place and cannot escape.

To keep the ball in the game's closing minutes, the players run out the clock. Airplanes use runways. So do fashion models.

Running lights are required by ships or aircraft traveling at night. A running knot is a slipknot. A running board is the footboard or step below a vehicle door.

If something is average or ordinary, it is run-of-the-mill. That manufacturing jargon refers to the material produced in the mill before its quality has been inspected and approved.

Run the gantlet and run the gamut are common expressions. "Run the gantlet" was originally a military punishment in which the victim was forced to run between two rows of people who beat him as he passed. The expression's figurative meaning is to be attacked or exposed to danger from all sides. (This expression is sometimes rendered "run the gauntlet," but a gauntlet is a glove — you "throw down the gauntlet" when challenging someone.)

"Run the gamut," which means a range or extent, derives from a musical scale or series of notes.

And there's always the long run and the short run. And the run of good luck or bad luck.

But that will do. Don't want to run it into the ground. Besides, I gotta run.

CHAPTER 18

PEOPLE LABELS

Let's forget for a moment all the reasons why we shouldn't label each other and observe that the labels we do use are often at least lazy and threadbare. Even those lovely words *conservative* and *liberal* carry so much emotional baggage that we've lost sight of the potential nobility they suggest: How nice to conserve. How nice to be open-handed.

We need fresh and imaginative words that identify people without being either meaningless or mean-spirited. And many such labels exist. We just don't use them. For example, we frequently talk about introverts and extraverts, but how do we identify those who are neither, those who balance sociability with healthy self-interest? There's a word for such people. It's *ambivert*.

Speaking of "ambi," we know what to call someone who is equally skillful with both hands. That person is *ambidextrous*. But what do we call someone who is equally *clumsy* with both hands? That person is *ambisinister*. "Ambi" is a prefix meaning both, and "sinister" means lefthandedness. So being ambisinister is a short form for saying we have two left hands.

What about people who have two left feet? No such word seems to exist, so let's play wordsmith and coin one.

Since "ped" means foot, what about *ambisiniped*? (A wordsmith, by the way, is a *logodaedalus*.)

What trait would you say the word *monoculist* identifies? It means to have only one eye. And speaking of eyes, are you a *presbyope*? Or a *myope*? If you're far-sighted, you're a presbyope, near-sighted, a myope — hence, the more commonly heard terms, presbyopia and myopia. But how might we label the near-sighted person who is lucky enough to have reached middle-age — and the age of the bifocal. Is that person a presbyopic myope?

Still speaking of eyes — are yours blue? And do you have blond hair? Then you're a *glaucope*. Now *there's* a label that sounds far more unattractive than the condition. No wonder we don't hear the term.

Or what if your eyes are brown instead of blue? Then you're a *cyanope* — a fair-haired, dark-eyed person. If you're a redhead, we can call you a *pyrrotist*. And if you have freckles with that red hair, you're a *lentiginous* pyrrotist. Sounds like something you could be arrested for, doesn't it?

We have fewer labels for thin people than we have for fat, and labels for skinnies are not as unflattering as those for chubbies. Of course, there are such terms: *beanpole, stringbean*, or *bag of bones*. Or the more clinical term *ectomorph*. But there's a finer, friendlier label for the naturally thin. It's *leptosome*. Compare that word to *porknell*, which labels a fat person and means not only a pig, but a *stuffed* pig.

This next label is probably one you can put to use immediately. Do you know people who wake to music, drive to work to music, fall asleep to music, and spend the rest of the time wearing headsets that pipe music directly into their ears? Those people are *melomaniacs*.

Bet you thought they had to be *some* kind of maniac, didn't you?

CHAPTER 19

SEEING RED

Sunday was a red-letter day, even if it had no special significance — at least according to many calendars.

"Red-letter" days began in the 1400s, and they were originally holy days, marked on the calendar in the church's colors of red or purple. That custom has survived six centuries — many calendars still mark Sundays in red, as well as holidays, descendants of "holy days."

Today, we've forgotten the red-letter day's connection to church and calendar and use the expression to refer to any day of special importance.

It's not surprising that red was a color of the church. Red, the color of our blood, always has played an important part in religion, ritual, myth, magic, and art. As the hottest and most aggressive color in the spectrum, red symbolizes not only blood, but also fire, urgency, alarm, warfare, and the radical or revolutionary. It's no wonder that "red-letter day" is just one of many popular "red" expressions. For starters: red as a beet, turn red, see red, red-blooded, red-eye, red-handed, red flag, red alert, red-pencil, a red mark against you, red ink, in the red, red light, red-light district, red cent, red carpet, red tape, red-neck, red herring, paint the town red.

Some of those expressions are self-explanatory — red

as a beet, for example. Some are tied to emotion — we see red in anger, turn red with embarrassment, and refer to someone strong, tough, or lusty as "red-blooded." A "red-eye" refers to a late- or all-night plane or train, which leaves passengers with bloodshot eyes from lack of sleep. "Red-handed" likewise relates to blood — we're caught in the act, with the figurative blood still on our hands.

"Red flag," a warning, and "red alert" are linked. "Red-pencil," meaning to edit or revise, is related to "a red mark against you," referring to the teacher's grading pen. "Red ink" or "in the red" are both connected to the accounting practice of entering negative amounts in red ink.

There's a world of difference, however, between "red light" and "red-light district."

"Red cent" refers to copper's reddish hue, and "red carpet" refers to the red runner guests tread at grand events. "Red tape" comes from 19th century British offices, where documents were bound in red ribbon and stowed (maybe to be forgotten) in cubbyholes or shelves. That red ribbon has come to symbolize bureaucratic regulation, delay, and inefficiency.

"Redneck" is a label suggesting bigotry and ignorance. It is usually applied to poor, white, rural Southerners — that sunburned neck comes from toiling in the fields.

"Red herring" means a false or misleading clue, scent, or decoy. When herring is smoked, it turns red, and "red herring" comes from the practice of dragging a smelly smoked herring over the ground to teach a dog to follow a scent. In days past, a savvy criminal being pursued by bloodhounds might drag a red herring (which apparently smelled stronger than the criminal) over his trail to cause the dogs to lose his scent.

"Paint the town red" means to go on a spree. Charles Funk surmises in his book *A Hog on Ice* that this expression originated when Indians on the warpath set a town on fire after killing its inhabitants — thereby "painting the town red." That seems a bit strained to me, and others disagree with Funk, noting that red has been tied to riotous behavior for many centuries.

When it comes to symbolic meaning, all other hues pale (pun intended), compared to red. Black and white make rich metaphors, but they aren't properly "colors." We have yellow dogs and bellies and journalism. We have blue collars and noses and moons. And we have green thumbs and lights and parties. But when you want metaphorical punch, put your money on red.

CHAPTER 20

TYPHOID MARY AND 'FRIENDS'

Who was Jack Robinson, anyway? And Davy Jones and Typhoid Mary? Why do we call a hot whiskey drink a "Tom and Jerry"? Was there really a Big Bertha? Who was George, of "Let George do it" fame? We toss around their names as though we knew. And we do understand intent, if not derivation.

Jack Robinson's origin is the least certain of this lot. He was apparently a mercurial fellow, though, since our expression is "as fast as you can say Jack Robinson." Some researchers attribute the expression to a ballad from the 1800s about a sailor named Jack Robinson. The ballad says he returned home after a long absence at sea and found his wife married to another. Rather than waste time brooding, though, he blessed his good luck and disappeared faster than you could say his name.

Davy Jones is just one of the many interesting epithets created by sea-going folk. Jones is a nautical devil and his locker the sailor's equivalent of Hell. Go to Davy Jones' locker and you go to the bottom of the sea. His name is a variant of *Jonah*, who brings bad luck to sailors. The Jonah myth, in turn, comes from the biblical account of Jonah's being swallowed by a whale — and his ghost, says the myth, snatches men's souls.

"Typhoid Mary" refers to Mary Mallon, an Irish immigrant who worked in New York as a cook around the turn of the century. We use the term "Typhoid Mary" to refer to people who spread disease or to identify a jinx.

Mary Mallon had a fascinating history. She was a carrier of typhoid fever, though she herself was immune to the disease. She singlehandedly caused an epidemic in the late 1800s, and the U.S. government prohibited her from working with food. The early 1900s brought another surge of typhoid fever, and health authorities once more traced the epidemic to Mary Mallon, who was again working as a cook — this time under an assumed name.

After the second epidemic, the government classified Mary Mallon a public menace and kept her both isolated and imprisoned for the rest of her life. She lived another 32 years and died in confinement in 1938.

Tom and Jerry have a lighter-hearted history. We use their names for a hot drink made with milk, egg and whiskey, and we also understand that the duo suggests rascality — as with Hanna Barbera's cartoon cat and mouse of the same names.

"Tom and Jerry" comes from British writer Pierce Egan, who wrote a popular chronicle in 1821 called "Life in London." The work was a record of two low-life rakes and revelers named — you guessed it. Egan's work brought forth a popular new expression — to "Tom and Jerry" it. When you "Tom and Jerried" it, you had a wild night out. Later, London dives came to be known as "Tom and Jerry shops" — and later still, just as "Jerry shops."

Big Bertha actually existed and not just as the long-range artillery weapon used in World War I. The gun was a showpiece rather than standard issue, but the Germans were so proud of it that they named it after Bertha Krupp, the grande dame of the Krupp munitions family. No word on what Bertha thought of the epithet.

The George of "Let George do it" fame was George Cardinal d'Amboise, prime minister of France under the incompetent Louis XII. When someone asked King Louis to do something, he said to "let George do it" with such frequency that the expression caught on as a pass-the-buck response to anything we don't want to do ourselves. The expression is still so current that a political lapel pin capitalizes on it — the button bears George W. Bush's likeness and the words "DON'T let George do it."

CHAPTER 21

WAR WORDS

Linguists and anthropologists say you can sometimes tell what's important in a culture by how many words that culture has for a subject. Eskimos, say, might have many words for snow, whereas capitalist cultures have many words for money.

War has contributed heavily to American English. We have so many war words, in fact, that lexicographer Christine Ammer compiled a dictionary of them. Her *Fighting Words* lists about 750 entries ranging from A to Z — *all quiet* to *zero hour,* say — and most of the words have been absorbed into the lexicon of common speech. The size of that vocabulary shows how important military action is in our society.

The roots of military terms are often obvious even when ancient. Both *skirmish* and *scrimmage* came from the medieval battlefield, for example. And the popular expression *avant-garde* is from the French, meaning the army's advance guard.

Some words born in military action have become so much a part of our everyday language, however, that their history is obscure if not hidden.

Screaming meemies, for example, came from the battlefields of World War I. Having the screaming meemies is like having the *heebie-jeebies* — that is, feeling edgy to the point of hysteria. The Yanks called certain German artillery shells screaming meemies because of their high-pitched squeal.

The term *baptism of fire* once referred to religious martyrs burned at the stake, but Napoleon made it a war term, writing that he loved the brave soldiers undergoing their "baptism of fire." Today, we use the term to refer to any first-time ordeal.

The word *deadline* did not originate in journalism as we might think, but in war, and it had nothing to do with the clock. During the Civil War, the deadline marked the inner stockade of a prison camp. Prisoners crossing that line were shot — hence, "dead line." Now, the term has come to mean any time limit.

We call a collarless sweater that buttons up the front a *cardigan,* so named for the Earl of Cardigan, a British cavalry officer. Notorious for incompetence, he led the charge of the Light Brigade. The soldiers may not have admired the man, but they admired his sweater — especially in the Crimean cold — and they too began wearing *cardigans* under their tunics.

Brinkmanship came from the Cold War during the '50s. Statesman Adlai Stevenson feared that Secretary of State John Foster Dulles' uncompromising stance with the Soviets was taking us to the *brink* of war. He termed Dulles' tactics *brinkmanship,* a term now used to identify risky negotiation.

Christine Ammer writes that some etymologists believe the military is responsible for the popular use of *hep* and its variant *hip*. *Hep* had been around since the early 1900s but came into common use during WWI to mean "with it." Experts speculate that the usage spread through the drill sergeant's "hep, hep, hep" marching count: The sergeant ordered an out-of-step soldier to "get hep."

If they're right, *hep's* variant *hip* made an interesting journey from war to peace — from WWI doughboys to pacifist *hippies*.

The military is famous for its acronyms and abbreviations. SOP for standard operating procedure, for example. AWOL for absent without leave, GI for government issue, VIP for very important person — all these soldierly expressions are solidly part of American English. R&R began as rest and recuperation and became rest and recreation. KP stands for kitchen police or patrol, C.O. for commanding officer. "Jeep" comes from the initials GP, for General Purpose Vehicle. The acronym SNAFU is both profane and well-known; we can purge the expletive and say it means *Situation Normal: All Fouled Up.*

Soldiers often borrow from the language of the enemy. *Blitz* and *flak* are shortened forms of longer German words: Blitz from *blitzkrieg*, which means, literally, "lightning war," and flak from *fliegerabwehrkanone*, a 19-letter wonder for anti-aircraft gun. Another commonly used word in our language, *honcho*, came from a Japanese word for "squad leader."

Snow job was a World War II invention. So was *Dear John, scuttlebutt, pin-up girl, airlift, shell-shock* and *smokescreen*. A *walkie-talkie* was a portable radio transmitter and receiver, a silly name that stuck and no longer seems silly. *Catch-22, tell that to the Marines, rising through the ranks* and *rank and file* are all military creations.

Domino theory is so firmly a part of our language that it's hard to believe it's as recent as the Vietnam era. Vietnam also brought us *defoliate, firefight, friendly fire* and *search-and-destroy. Brainwashing* and *chopper* came from the Korean War. *Gunboat diplomacy* is older — from the '20s. *Foxhole* has been with us since World War I. So has *graveyard shift*, a term coined when shipbuilders and munitions workers labored around the clock. Such terms as *war horse, about face* and *hold the fort* are older still, deriving from the Civil War.

As you might guess, many new words moved into general use after Hiroshima and Nagasaki. Among them are *mushroom cloud, countdown, fireball, test site, chain reaction, fission, fusion* and *fallout*. The post-Hiroshima period gave us *Cold War*. The expression *Bamboo Curtain* came in turn from Winston Churchill's coinage, *Iron Curtain*.

We can't be sure yet which new terms will come from the Gulf War or the war in Iraq. The ridiculous euphemism *collateral damage*, which means killing civilians, seems an unlikely candidate. But we can be sure that our military efforts against Saddam Hussein will make some contribution to our vocabulary. War means drama and devastation; it's bound to leave its mark not only on the people and the land, but also on the language.

CHAPTER 22

TOM SWIFTIE

People who love words usually love word play. That often means word games, whether Scrabble or crossword puzzles or other brain teasers such as acrostics or anagrams. And word lovers usually — whether they admit it or not — like puns.

One word game that even children can play is the Tom Swiftie, so named from the Tom Swift adventure stories of the 1920s. Many young people, especially boys, grew up reading about Tom Swift, a noble young hero created by Edward Stratemeyer. The Tom Swiftie, also called an adverbial pun, spoofs the habit of Swift characters never to simply *say* anything. Rather, they say it excitedly, sadly, happily, loudly — you get the idea.

The Tom Swiftie makes that adverb a pun on the statement itself. For example: "The stock market is going through the roof!" Tom said *bullishly*. Or: "Who ate all the apples?" asked Tom, *fruitlessly*. That's the basic Tom Swiftie. Here are some others:

"I just drank a whole pot of coffee," said Tom perkily.

"She made fake turtle soup," said Tom mockingly.

"I'm going to cash in my chips," said Tom winningly.

"My pencil lead is broken," said Tom pointlessly.

"I hate the taste of unsweetened chocolate," said Tom

bitterly.

"I have to visit the cemetery," said Tom cryptically.

"Be sure to put plenty of starch in my shirts," said Tom stiffly.

"I can't find my CD player," said Tom tunelessly.

"Could I have some of that dark bread?" asked Tom wryly.

"They'll never guess I made this basket myself," said Tom craftily.

"I'm sort of fond of modern art," said Tom abstractly.

"Those atomic tests were something!" said Tom glowingly.

Some Tom Swifties depend upon the names of well-known businesses or products. Here are examples of that sort of Swiftie:

"I forgot my toothpaste!" said Tom, crestfallen.

"Are we eating at McDonald's *again*?" asked Tom archly.

"I wish we had some pineapple," said Tom dolefully.

"Hey, we're out of laundry detergent," said Tom cheerlessly.

Another kind of Tom Swiftie is a pun in which the verb — rather than an adverb — provides the humor. That kind of Swiftie usually focuses on the verb of attribution:

"Hey, get this dog off me," Tom barked.

"My oil well just came in!" Tom gushed.

"Where's my bullfrog?" Tom croaked.

"Can't you darn your own socks?" Tom needled.

Yet another kind of Tom Swiftie — and the most challenging — is the double Swiftie. In this sort of Swiftie, both the verb and the adverb are puns. For example: "How did I do on my final exam?" Tom quizzed testily. Here are a few more double Swifties:

"That dog is nothing but a mongrel," Tom muttered doggedly.

"I love sweet potatoes," Tom yammered starchily.

"This meat is so tough!" Tom beefed jerkily.

Word play of all kinds is not only fun and funny, it's especially valuable to children and young people. Something as elementary as the Tom Swiftie can help them appreciate words and how words work. It also can enlarge their imaginations as well as their vocabularies. But the best thing about such word play is any age can play.

CHAPTER 23

TRICKY WORDS

Provide the words that answer the questions below. (Hint: The answer to Number 8 names a column in this book.) Answers follow.

1. A person named for someone is called that someone's *namesake*. What do you call the person for whom one is named?

2. What do you call the metal or plastic covering on the end of a shoelace?

3. Consider the hole through which you pass a shoelace. What do you call the metal or plastic ring that reinforces that hole?

4. Name a seven-letter word that contains all five vowels (*a, e, i, o, u*).

5. Name a word in which the vowels *a, e, i, o,* and *u* appear once, and in that order.

6. Name a word in which those five vowels appear once,

but in reverse order *(u, o, i, e, a)*.

7. What do you call a word or phrase that reads the same forward and backward? For example: *Madam, I'm Adam.*

8. What do you call a slip of tongue that humorously transposes the sounds of two or more words? For example, intending to say "sons of toil," and saying instead "tons of soil." Or intending to say, "The flags were hung out," and saying instead, "The hags were flung out."

9. What do you call a humorous confusion of one word with another — for example, saying "vanilla folder" instead of "*manila* folder." Or "polo bears" instead of "*polar* bears." Or "extinguished" instead of *distinguished.*

10. What do you call a word that derives from a place — for example, *shanghai* (to put aboard a ship through force or trickery).

11. What do you call a word or expression that derives from a part of the body — for example, a *nose* for news, *toe* the line, a pain in the *neck*?

12. What do you call a symbol such as this: :-) or this: [:-o?

ANSWERS

1. The person or thing someone or something is named for is an *eponym.*

2. The tip on a lace that keeps the lace from raveling is an *aglet*.

3. The metal or plastic ring that reinforces the hole through which a lace passes is a *grommet*.

4. *Sequoia* is a seven-letter word that contains all five vowels.

5. Three words in which the vowels *a, e, i, o,* and *u* appear once and in that order: *facetious* (teasing, not serious); *abstemious* (temperate, austere, frugal); *aerious* (airy).

6. Two words in which the vowels *a, e, i, o,* and *u* appear once, in reverse order: *subcontinental, uncomplimentary.*

7. A *palindrome* reads the same forward and backward. The word *palindrome* is derived from the Greek *palíndromos*, which means "running back again." Examples: *Radar. Level. Civic. Noon. Racecar.*

8. A *spoonerism* transposes sounds. The eponym for this linguistic faux pas was the Rev. William Spooner, who once said when toasting the queen, "Here's to our queer old dean." (More on spoonerisms in Part Two: Words and the Calendar.)

9. Humorously confusing one word with another is a *malapropism*. The eponym for this error is Mrs. Malaprop, a character in a 1775 play by Richard Sheridan, "The

Rivals." Mrs. Malaprop referred, for example, to "allegories" instead of *alligators*.

10. A word that derives from a place is a *toponym*. Timbuktu, for example, is an actual city in Africa, but we use the word to refer to any faraway or inaccessible spot: "I didn't know I would have to drive to Timbuktu to go to this party."

11. A word that derives from a part of the body is an *anatonym*.

12. Symbols such as the smiling or frowning face are called *emoticons*, cyberspeak for "emotion icons." Emoticons are typed from the computer's keyboard — the smiling face :-) is created by typing colon, hyphen, and parenthesis. Certain emoticons are so common that some software programs include them as symbols that can be inserted into the document.

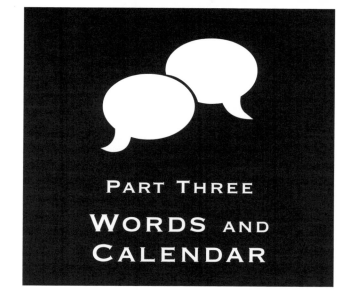

PART THREE

WORDS AND CALENDAR

CHAPTER 24

THE EQUINOX

This morning, the sun crossed the equator — so quietly you may not have noticed — and ushered in the first day of spring.

We term this crossing the "vernal equinox" — *vernal* for spring, and *equinox* for "equal night" because it's one of two times a year that days and nights are equal in length all over the earth. The other equinox this year will occur Sept. 22 and will herald fall, at least for those north of the equator. (South of the equator, the seasons are reversed, with the March equinox announcing autumn and the

September equinox heralding spring.)

Of the two, the March equinox gets most of our attention, probably because, for us, it says goodbye to winter and hello to spring. No season is more welcome than spring. It has had special significance from the earliest times as the season of rebirth and reawakening — both actually and symbolically.

This morning's equinox also opened a stretch of time termed "springtide" — a word that in itself suggests sweep and movement. Springtide comprises March, April and May and extends to the June *solstice*, a term deriving from the Latin roots *sol*, meaning "sun," and *sisto,* to "stop" or "stand still." Like the equinox, the solstice occurs twice a year — when the sun is farthest from the equator and seems, in a sense, to stand still.

Calling the season that opened today "spring" is an old if not ancient practice in English. This sense of *spring* comes from the notion of plants "springing up," shown in references from the 1300s to the "springing times" and from the 1500s to the "spring of the leaf."

Middle English even had its equivalent of our "spring chicken": *springald* or *springal,* which meant a young man or stripling. In the late 1700s, "spring chicken" meant a young chicken, usually 11 to 14 weeks old, and the term gained the metaphorical meaning of "young person" in the early 1900s.

We see the sense of restless revamping and renewing in such expressions as spring cleaning, spring training, spring break, spring fever. Spring as a time of unleashing energies pent up over a long winter is a concept handed down from our ancient forebears and their spring rites, celebrations and myths. We say "wild as a March hare" — referring to the mating-season behavior of the hare, an ancient symbol of fertility.

March was the first month of the year in the Roman calendar predating Julius Caesar. The month opened not only the year and spring and the season for planting, but also the season for making war. Hence, March takes its name from Mars, god of war.

The Old English name for March was "Hyld-Monath," which means "boisterous month" — presumably because of the winds. It seems appropriate that the month engendering spring cleaning is also the windy month. I've always thought of March as nature's way to "spring clean," by dusting the rooftops, pulling down dead leaves and branches, and sweeping the earth of winter's debris.

Like us, our Old English forebears also suffered spring fever. Their incredible word for that dreamy, distracted state was *lenctenadle*.

And you, too, may be feeling especially restless and yearning right now. But, to paraphrase Irving Berlin: There is nothing you can take to relieve that pleasant ache — you're not sick, you're just in lenctenadle.

CHAPTER 25

MARCH: MONTH OF BLUSTER

March, like other months, has its share of official calendar observances, some of them surprisingly zany. Many of the days we memorialize have serious intent or are at least well known. There's the vernal equinox or first day of spring, of course, which we discussed in the previous column — as well as Ides of March Day on March 15 and St. Patrick's Day on March 17.

But what about St. Urho Day, which is March 16, the day before St. Patrick's Day? As you might guess, it honors St. Urho, the patron saint of Finland, who supposedly used his huge and splendid voice to chase grasshoppers out of pre-Ice Age Finland — thus saving the grape harvest. This was when the climate was much milder.

I should tell you that St. Urho was apparently invented in the 1950s by a couple of Minnesota Finns as a joke. But American Finns love him just the same. And now St. Urho Day is taken seriously enough that it's officially recognized in all 50 states. You can even buy St. Urho Day greeting cards.

The Irish, for their part, claim that the whole Urho affair was an attempt by the Finns not only to preempt their holiday, but their beer — which the Finns dye purple instead of green, to honor the grape.

March is one of many months rich in both sublime *and* ridiculous official month-long observances. Not only is it the National Women's History Month, Red Cross Month, Save Your Vision Month, and National Nutrition Month, it's also International Mirth Month, National Caffeine Awareness Month, National Frozen Food Month, National Umbrella Month, and National Noodle Month.

March also has its week-long observances. For example, there's National Bubble Gum Week, the second week in March, *and* National Bubble Blowers' Week, which runs from the 20th to the 27th and which I completely forgot. Maybe you did, too. But there's also National Procrastination Week, which some of us try to celebrate all year long. And American Chocolate Week, which some of us *do* celebrate all year long.

March also provides plenty of daily observances throughout the month. March 1, for example, is National Peanut Butter Lovers Day, Beer Day, and Pig Day. Don't want to forget those! And March 22 is National Common Courtesy Day, March 9 is Panic Day, and March 15 is True Confessions Day. After Beer Day and Pig Day, we might need those.

March 5 is Multiple Personalities Day. Shouldn't that be more than one day?

It may be in observance of March as National Nutrition Month that we have Potato Chip Day on March 14, Toast Day on March 23, Chocolate Covered Raisins Day on March 24, and Tater Day on March 31.

Or best, maybe, in terms of nutrition: Something on a Stick Day, which is March 28.

You think I'm kidding, don't you? But I'm not. You

think I'm going to shout *April Fool,* don't you? But I'm not. We observe *that* day on April 1.

But wouldn't it be perfect if April Fool's Day occurred in March?

CHAPTER 26

SHAKESPEARE'S BIRTHDAY

This week will mark the anniversaries of both the birth and death of William Shakespeare. The consensus of experts is that he was born April 23, 1564, and died on April 23, 1616 — his birthday.

Four hundred-plus years is a long time to be the English language's leading poet and wordsmith. By "wordsmith," I suggest not only the beauty and profundity of Shakespeare's prose, but also its freshness and originality. Shakespeare frequently drew his dramas from old and oft-told tales, but he made them new again through his creative vision and inventive phrasing.

The same is true of his language. Whatever his meaning, Shakespeare had the right word for it. And if he didn't, he created it. His countless linguistic inventions thrive in everyday speech all these years later and are so much a part of the language that they often are springboards to fresh coinage. For example, his "to the manner born" — meaning accustomed to the elegance of manners — generated the witty title of British TV's "To the Manor Born." The stock market embellished Shakespeare's "witching hour," making it "triple-witching hour" — the unpredictable trading preceding the simultaneous expiration of three kinds of stock options.

Any number of other popular expressions from Shakespeare enrich today's idiom: Salad days. Over hill, over dale. Middle of the night. Quiet as a lamb. Motley fool. Eating me out of house and home. Laid on with a trowel. Forgive and forget. Sweets to the sweet. Elbow room. Naked truth. Charmed life. A dish fit for the gods. Sink or swim. Brave new world. Men of few words. Not a mouse stirring. Forever and a day.

Shakespeare gave us myriad individual words as well. Here are a few whose first recorded use were in Shakespeare's works: lustrous, immediacy, design, mimic, pander, quarrelsome, critic, besmirch, reword, misquote.

That's a tiny fraction of Shakespeare's original contribution to the English lexicon.

In focusing on the clarity, beauty, and originality of what Shakespeare *would* say, however, we fail to mention what he *wouldn't* say. He would not traffic in the faux cleverness of mimicry, and he wouldn't indulge in the trite and unthinking expression that clogs so much communication today.

He wouldn't, for example, go for it, check it out, chill out, kick back, or take a chill pill. He wouldn't utilize, finalize, maximize, strategize, or prioritize. He wouldn't interface, offer input, or ask for feedback. He wouldn't relate, validate, or identify with.

He wouldn't be *into* or *about* anything. He wouldn't parent, bond, or nurture. He'd skip quality time and meaningful dialogue. He wouldn't get a life or have a lifestyle, a learning experience, a meaningful relationship, a growth period, or a mid-life crisis. He wouldn't office, conference, dialogue with, do lunch, cocoon, or be a couch potato.

Shakespeare wouldn't get horizontal or get naked. He wouldn't be a homeboy, a main man, or a main squeeze. He wouldn't call anyone a beautiful person, a people person, a class act, or a happy camper. He wouldn't add "or what" to questions such as: "Is this a great country, or what?" He wouldn't say WONNNderful, hopefully, super, déjà vu, or happenin'. He'd skip totally, basically, arguably, and parameter. He wouldn't say doable or winnable. He'd think twice before he wrote venue or resonate. And he'd never, ever say proactive.

He wouldn't discuss which options were on the table, bottom lines, or worst-case scenarios. He wouldn't try to send a signal. He wouldn't disemploy, dehire, or debrief. He wouldn't create disincentives. He wouldn't waste anybody, take anybody out, or blow anybody away.

And should William Shakespeare sit quill in hand, contemplating the terms that now pass for fresh, lively, or creative expression, he wouldn't say: "Hey, dude, no prob. I can live with that. Have a nice day."

CHAPTER 27

FOR THE FATHERS

We have celebrated Father's Day for nearly a century, yet this tribute became an official national holiday only in 1966, when President Lyndon Johnson signed a proclamation declaring the third Sunday in June Father's Day. Even later — in 1972 — Richard Nixon signed a law making Father's Day a permanent observance.

The first Father's Day was celebrated in Spokane, Wash., in 1910. The commemoration was the creation of Sonora Dodd, whose father, William Smart, was a farmer who was widowed and raised his six young children alone. As an adult, Sonora Dodd realized how selfless and courageous her father had been, and she wanted to thank him and all such fathers.

She chose June for the first Father's Day because it was William Smart's birth month.

In preserving, protecting, and nurturing his family, William Smart not only did what good fathers do, but he also did what the word "father" means.

"Father" has been an English word for as long as there has been an English language — and its root predates English by untold centuries. How do we know? Because it came from the Indo-European tongue, a major taproot for English. The word's form and pronunciation changed as

Indo-European branched into different languages, but root and meaning stayed the same.

Simply stated, *father* descends from the Indo-European word for father, *pater,* which incorporates the ancient root *pa,* meaning to feed and protect. From this same source came various forms — the Greek and Latin *pater,* the Sanskrit *pitar,* the Old English *faeder,* the Germanic *fader,* the English *father.* The Indo-European *pater* became *father* because a consonant shift in the Germanic branch of Indo-European changed P to F, and T to TH. (The P to F shift is seen, for example, in the P of *pyr* — as in *pyromaniac* or funeral *pyre* — becoming the F of the Germanic *fire.*)

So such renderings of *father* as *fater, fader* or *fadre* share the same root and meaning as the Latin *pater,* Spanish *padre,* Greek *pappas,* and French *pere.* And whether transcribed as P or F, that ancient *pa* root denoted food or foodgiver in languages sharing Indo-European roots — extending logically over time to mean protector, progenitor, teacher, counselor, and the like.

From this root also came the Germanic *food, fodder* and *forage,* and the Greek *foster.* In Latin (the consonant shift generally was not seen in Romance languages), it generated *panis,* meaning food; *pascere,* to feed; *panarium,* breadbasket; and *pasture. Pan, panne* and *pain* mean bread in different languages. The English have *pasties,* the Americans *pastries,* and the French *pattisseries.* We cook in *pans,* and we keep food in the English *pantry,* the French *paneterie,* the Latin *paneteria.*

A re*past* is a meal, and anti*pasto* is what we eat "before the meal." *Pamper* originally meant to feed too much.

Patriarch, *paternal*, *patron*, *pastor* and *pope* also derive from this root and denote fatherly benefactors. The *Paternoster*, the Lord's Prayer, literally means "our father."

So: Happy Father's Day to all you paters and papas who feed your brood — not just daily bread, but food for the heart and mind as well. You are a blessing in what you do and in what you teach, as basic and indispensable to our culture as your name is to our language. As the proverb declares: "One father is more than a hundred schoolmasters."

CHAPTER 28

YANKEE DOODLE DAY

Next week, we'll celebrate the Fourth of July — a holiday as American as hot dogs, hamburgers, barbecues, potato chips, and Yankee Doodle Dandy.

In short, as American as apple pie.

Apple pie is called the country's first culinary specialty — Americans have baked bits of apple in crusts since the earliest colonial days. But Allan Metcalf and David Barnhart write in *America in So Many Words* that Americans "cannot claim to have invented the apple pie, just to have perfected it." The authors note that apple pie was common as early as 1697, when one Samuel Sewall of Boston wrote in his diary that he'd had a picnic meal of "rost lamb, turkey, fowls, applepy."

Maybe we also "perfected" what we now call dogs and burgers. We borrowed from the Germans the "frankfurter" — a sausage also called a "wiener" or "red hot." The name "hot dog" is wholly American, however. Metcalf and Barnhart recount that in the 1800s, a popular joke (which many believed) was that sausage meat was dog meat. By mid-century, those maligned sausages were placed in narrow buns and sold from lunch wagons — cheap and fast fare for students, who began calling the sausages "hot dogs." By the late 1800s, hot dogs were known by that name everywhere, and the canine connection no longer disturbed anyone.

The hamburger, too, was borrowed from Germany and has, as you know, nothing to do with ham. It came from the German city of Hamburg. Also like the hot dog, the hamburger dates to the late 1800s, when Americans began forming ground beef into patties and frying them. By the early 1900s, the patties were showing up in compact and convenient round buns, and the result was on its way to becoming the king of American fast food. "Cheeseburgers" appeared in the 1930s, and the prefix "ham" became superfluous. Now we have any number of "burgers" — chiliburgers, soyburgers, veggieburgers.

Barbecuing has been popular in America for centuries, but it, too, is an import. Spanish explorers brought the barbecue to American shores, write Metcalf and Barnhart. The explorers had observed Haiti's Tainu Indians drying and roasting animals on raised frames over fire, and such outdoor cookery became a common social event on America's Atlantic coast as early as the mid-1700s.

If dogs, burgers, and barbecues were borrowed, potato chips are as American as the American Indian who first created them. The country's favorite snack also has an interesting history, related in Charles Panati's *Extraordinary Origins of Everyday Things*.

In the mid-1800s, George Crum, a Native American chef at an elegant lodge in Saratoga, New York, created "Saratoga chips" — not in a flash of inspiration but in a fit of pique. An illustrious lodge guest, Cornelius Vanderbilt, had repeatedly complained that Crum's french fries were too thick. After several offerings of ever-thinner slices of potato, an annoyed Chef Crum finally sliced the potatoes razor-thin before frying them in hot fat, figuring they'd be too thin and crisp to stab with a fork and would thereby shut up the ornery guest. But Vanderbilt and other diners loved the salty, golden-brown, paper-thin potatoes, and the popularity of Saratoga Chips spread to other parts of the country, losing their "Saratoga" label along the way and becoming just "potato chips," the quintessential American snack food.

"Yankee" is an old word with a colorful and varied history. Its origin is fuzzy, but according to H. L. Mencken's *American Language*, it probably came from the Dutch Jan Kaas, a term Europeans used for centuries to identify a Hollander. Jan (pronounced "yahn") is Dutch for John, and Janke ("yahnky") is its diminutive. In the late 1600s, a Dutch commander in the West Indies became known as "Captain Yankey," and *yankey* came to mean pirates or piracy. English buccaneers used such expressions to refer to Dutch freebooters, so the terms were commonplace in New York.

By the mid-1700s, *yankey* and *yankee* — still a derogatory term — had come to mean a New Englander. But to the British, the term included all American "provincials." The silly song "Yankee Doodle Dandy," which described a fool, was written by a British Army surgeon to deride American troops. The cocky "Yankee" troops weren't bothered in the least, however, and during the Revolution, they proudly adopted "Yankee Doodle Dandy" for their marching song.

The word Yankee narrowed during the Civil War to become a slur against the North, but widened yet again during World Wars I and II, when Southerners who might object to being called Yankees were nevertheless proud to be called Yanks.

So happy Fourth to you, fellow Yanks. It's a feather in our caps, even if we call it macaroni.

CHAPTER 29

SPOONERISMS

I handed a colleague something to read and said, to her amusement: "Weed it and reap."

It happens to everyone from time to time, that accidental switching of letters or syllables. A weatherman warns of impending "slow and sneet." A friend says not to put the "course before the heart." Another refers to a "trickup puck."

My husband once referred to Battle Creek, Michigan — the "cereal city" — as the land of "pop, snackle, and crap."

We call such gaffes "spoonerisms," after William Archibald Spooner, whose birthday is this month. The Rev. Spooner was born in London in July 1844 and died in 1930. He was a brilliant Anglican priest and scholar. His distinguished career included a 60-year association with Oxford University — not only as a lecturer in history, philosophy and divinity, but also as dean for more than a decade and as president for more than two.

The Rev. Spooner's brain was apparently more nimble than his tongue, though, because we remember him not so much for his scholarship as for what he himself might have called his "tips of the slung."

Those slips of the tongue are legendary not only

because they were so frequent, but also because they were so *funny*. His transpositions often yielded more than simple nonsense — they sometimes created other words and other, unintended meanings. For example, he once scolded an errant student: "You hissed my mystery lecture." He also praised a country cottage not as a "cozy little nook," but as a "nosy little crook." And on a visit to a dean's office, he asked the secretary: "Is the bean dizzy?"

Some have said that the Rev. Spooner could not possibly have committed all the spoonerisms attributed to him. But he himself acknowledged many of them. He said he once meant to tell a congregation to sing the hymn "Conquering Kings Their Titles Take." It came out "Kinkering Congs Their Titles Take."

Many of the Rev. Spooner's trademark slips came from the pulpit. For example, he told the congregation: "Our Lord is a shoving leopard." He changed "For now we see through a glass, darkly," to "through a dark, glassly." And he informed a student audience after one Sunday service: "In the sermon I have just preached, whenever I said Aristotle, I meant St. Paul."

But he didn't have to be in the pulpit to twist his words. Finding someone sitting in his church seat, he said politely: "Sir, I believe you're occupewing my pie." Then he added helpfully: "May I sew you to another sheet?" And while performing a wedding ceremony, he told the groom: "Son, it is now kisstomary to cuss the bride."

The Rev. Spooner also praised the country's farmers as "tons of soil." Describing the celebration at the end of WWI, the Reverend said that the "hags were all flung out." And, raising his glass to honor Queen Victoria with a toast to the "dear old queen," he cried instead: "Three cheers for the queer old dean!"

The term *spoonerism* is mildly amusing in its own right. And it's easier to remember than *metathesis*, which is what we called such linguistic switches before William Spooner practiced his particular talent for them. So we have a couple of reasons to thank the Rev. Spooner — not only for his bequest of bloopers, but also for lending them his nunny fame.

CHAPTER 30

SEIZE THE (DOG) DAY

As a child, I thought the expression "dog days" had to do with dogs. After all, dogs were usually consigned to the out-of-doors and, in the full of summer, lolled about listlessly. Or went mad from rabies. I also knew that all dogs have their days and thought maybe dog days were some of them.

Nothing of the sort.

The dog in "dog days" is not a dog at all, but a star — Sirius, the Dog Star. During the dog days — July and August in the northern hemisphere — Sirius rises and sets with the sun. The ancients thought that the combined heat of the sun and this bright star caused the sweltering weather. So the Dog Star, not Fido, is the star in that old expression.

The word "day" is itself linked to heat. It derives from the same ancient root that appears in the Sanskrit word *dah*, meaning "to burn." One might think the essence of day would be closer to light than to heat, but the word's early ancestor came from a place where daylight was synonymous with a fiery sun. Eventually, the roots of our word *day* passed from Sanskrit to the Germanic tongues, to Old English (*dæg*), and to Middle English (*dai*), later developing its current spelling.

Salad days and halcyon days are two more old but common "day" expressions. Salad days refers to when we were "green" — when we were young, innocent, and untried. Shakespeare writes in Antony and Cleopatra: "My salad days, when I was green in judgment."

Halcyon days were once real instead of figurative — real enough to be on the ancient calendar. The halcyon days occurred around the winter solstice and represented a period of peace and tranquility. The halcyon was a legendary bird that had the power to still the wind and thus to calm the seas. It supposedly sat on its nest in the sea during the halcyon days, and by quieting the wind, protected its nest from waves. Today, we use the term "halcyon days" to refer to any idyllic period of peace and calm.

It's no surprise that *day*, which defines most of our waking hours, is one of our ever-present metaphors. We have Day One. We have the Day of Judgment and the Day of Atonement. We have all the livelong day, forever and a day, and from this day forward. We have mayday, payday, heyday, rainy day, doom's day, an apple a day, and the day of infamy. We have our day in court, and we win the day, or we call it a day. We have a cold day in Hell. We have the days of auld lang syne, days of grace, and days of wine and roses. We rue the day that Rome wasn't built in a day. Charles Lamb wrote in 1823 that the "red-letter days" had become "dead-letter days."

But, after all, as Scarlett O'Hara said, tomorrow is another day. Besides, on a clear day, you can see forever. It's the end of a perfect day, and happy days are here again. Any day now.

Meantime, here we are, deep in dog day. Or wash day. Or bad hair day. Whatever, go ahead and make my day. Carpe diem.

CHAPTER 31

MONTH MONIKERS

It's September, and the autumn weather turns the leaves to flame. And while we're wondering whether we have time to play the waiting game, let's wonder, too, why the last four months of the year have such bland monikers. Eight of the months bear romantic or at least imaginative names, but the last four months seem to have been named by bean-counters.

September gets its name from the Latin *septem*, which means seven. For us, of course, September is the ninth month. But before the Gregorian calendar made January the first month, the year began in March. So September was indeed the seventh month.

October, November and December are equally bland. Those names are from the Latin *octo, novem* and *decem* — predictably, eight, nine and ten.

Maybe those namers ran out of good ideas. Or maybe they were just taking the safer course. They had named July and August after two Caesars and were being pressured by other important people to name months after them, too. Maybe they thought it more politic to stick to neutral labels. So they assigned numbers to a few months, then named a handful after gods, who — despite their reputation — may have seemed less likely to strike back.

January comes from the god Janus, an ancient deity who guarded entrances and exits. He had two faces, one that looked forward and one that looked back. And January can be seen as a pivotal month, one that looks to both past and future. The word *janitor* comes from this same root — a janitor does in a sense guard the doors.

February is from the Latin *februaria*, originally a time of expiation and purification. The month marked an ancient Roman ceremony in which infertile women were "purified" by being struck with goat-hide whips called *februa*.

March comes from Mars, the god of war, and is so named because March was the season-opener for doing battle. Again, the first of the year occurred in March: The 25th, which marked the vernal equinox and was therefore the first day of spring, also was New Year's Day. (In very early times, the Church of Rome regarded March 25, not 21, as the equinox.)

April, however, was the first full month of the year. *April* comes from the Roman god Aprilis, whose name in turn derives from a root meaning *open*. The month's ancient sense of *opener* lends poetic irony to T.S. Eliot's "April is the cruellest month, breeding lilacs out of the dead land."

Our fifth month derives from the mother goddess Maia. May is known as the lusty month, and in ancient times, it also honored chastity. It's considered an unlucky month for marriage, maybe because of its confusing connection to both lust and chastity.

Experts generally agree that the name *June* comes from the god Juno, protector of women. June has been a bride's preferred month for marriage since the Roman Empire, and the month's association with Juno would explain that preference.

Mark Antony named July. He suggested naming the month after Julius Caesar; then Octavian, the first Roman emperor, jealously insisted on having his own month as well. Octavian's month was christened "August" after Octavian's official title of Augustus Caesar.

Before the English adopted the Gregorian calendar, however, the months had other names — old English names that reflected their Germanic roots as well as the plain and practical nature of the Germanic breed.

For example, the month we call January was in old English *Wulf-Monath* — or wolf-month. There was a good chance of seeing wolves at that time because they ventured closer to villages during the cold.

February's old name was protypically Germanic. It was *Sprote-kalemonath* and meant, literally, cabbage-sprouting month.

March was *Hlyd-Monath* — meaning boisterous month, because of March winds. And April was *Easter-Monath*, meaning Easter month.

The month that became May was *Thri-milce Monath,* because the days were getting long enough to milk the cows three times.

The old English name for June was *Sere-Monath* or dry month. July was *Maed-Monath* or meadow month. And August was a matter-of-fact *Woed-Monath* or weed month.

September was, predictably, *Haerfest-Monath*, meaning harvest month.

Regarding October, we can best quote writer Doris

Lessing: "But what of October, that ambiguous month, the month of tension, the unendurable month?" October was *Win-Monath,* or wine month. That should help!

November was *Blot-Monath.* And if that sounds like blood month, it's no surprise, because the words mean sacrifice month. Non-Christian Anglo Saxons sacrificed cattle to their gods in November.

And December was the pedestrian *Mid-Winter-Monath*, meaning you-know-what.

So if we'd kept the old calendar, those are the names we'd have today. New Year's Day would fall on the first of wolf month. Now *there's* an omen. Mother's Day would be the second Sunday of three-milkings month and Father's Day would be in dry month. Unintentional symbolism, surely.

For Thanksgiving, we'd give more than thanks because it would be sacrifice month.

The 4th of July would be the 4th of meadow month. Doesn't sound like much of a blow-out, does it? And St. Patrick's Day would fall on the 17th of boisterous month, which sounds about right.

And the most *romantic* day, the day set aside for lovers, would fall on the 14th of Cabbage-sprouting month.

So let's hear it for the Gregorian calendar. What we *could* have had makes even the bean-counter names of September, October, November, and December sound romantic.

CHAPTER 32

WORDS TO GIVE THANKS BY

We've all heard the origin of our day of Thanksgiving: Plymouth Colony had a good harvest in 1621, and Gov. William Bradford declared a day of thanks for the bounty. The festive occasion included a feast for the whole community, including neighboring Indians.

Through the years, that celebration was repeated sporadically after successful harvests, but early Americans didn't observe it annually until more than a century and a half later, when George Washington proclaimed a national Day of Thanks on Nov. 26, 1789. Even then, the event was not firmly on the calendar until more than seven decades later, when Abraham Lincoln declared Thanksgiving a national holiday.

Three of the colonials' staples are staples of Thanksgiving tradition as well: turkey, cranberries, and pumpkin pie. It's appropriate that we enjoy pumpkin pie on this most American holiday — it, more than apple, should be the pie things are supposed to be "as American as." Pumpkin pie was a dish from the colonies, present in colonial writings as early as 1654 — well before the first recorded mention of apple pie (1697, according to Allan Metcalf and David Barnhart's *America in So Many Words*), which was created elsewhere in any case. The saying "as

American as apple pie" wasn't in wide use until the latter half of the 20th century.

Cranberries, however, were well known on both sides of the Atlantic in colonial times. To the Indians, the berries were *sassamanesh*. The British knew them variously as *fen berries, marsh berries, moss berries, marsh whorts,* or *fen whorts.* (Fen whorts. Yum.)

So why do we call them *cranberries*? According to Metcalf and Barnhart, the name came from the Dutch of New Amsterdam. Germans had their *kranbeere*, and the Dutch had their *kronbere* or *kranebere*. Those words mean "crane-berry," probably referring to the fact that cranes ate the berry in its European bogs — although some say the shape of the cranberry stem resembles a crane.

But the big word come Thursday will be the big bird: *turkey*. The star of Turkey Day has a stage name, however. The early colonials mistook the bird they found in America for the "turkey" known in England during the 1500s, write Metcalf and Barnhart. The bird in England, however, was from Guinea, Africa, and was a different species from the large native game bird found in America. The name *turkey* came from the fact that the African bird came to England by way of Turkey. Eventually it was understood that the American and African birds were unrelated, however, and to avoid confusion, the African bird became the "guinea fowl."

That early confusion is still reflected in the birds' scientific names, though, writes Charles Funk in *Horsefeathers,* because they share the label *meleagris*.

Mistaken identity aside, the word *turkey* plays multiple roles in American English. We call a poor stage or film production a *turkey*, for example, and we give the same name to a bumbling or inadequate person. We "talk turkey" when we're candid and direct — possibly because of the bird's bold, constant, and seemingly contentious gobble.

When we suddenly quit a habit, we call it going "cold turkey" — a term that comes from the world of drug addiction. When addicts, especially heroin addicts, quit cold turkey, the withdrawal directs the blood to the internal organs, leaving the skin pale and "chill-bumped" — like turkey flesh.

The turkey — both bird and word — deserves a special salute. Whatever else it is, it's as American as pumpkin pie.

CHAPTER 33

TIME RUNNING OUT

A friend examined her December calendar and complained: *There's too much happening!*

The clock seems to run faster toward the end of the year — especially during the holidays. Our general sense of hurry is heightened by warnings from the media and Madison Avenue that we haven't much time left. We have only a month. Then a few weeks. Then a handful of days. And, suddenly, it's the *eleventh hour.* We might get in just *under the wire* if we make a *last-ditch effort.*

An ad proclaims that one item has been marked down "in the St. Nick of time" and another item "just in time for Xmas." That "St. Nick of time," although not very effective word play, suggests how humankind once thought of time — as mechanistic rather than flowing.

The "nick of time" is an ancient expression — at least three centuries old. It means at the last minute. Originally, the expression was simply "in the nick" or "in the notch." When this expression came into being, time was thought of loosely as a metaphorical wheel or belt with notches or nicks that could receive a cog. Time moved in that exact and mechanical way — the wheel or belt turned, and the moment of turning was "in the very nick." With time so precisely notched, one also might act "in the nick."

Today we tend to think of time as a river rather than as a machine — we "go with the flow."

Not only is that ad interesting because of its "St. Nick" word play, but also because of its use of "Xmas," a once-common construction. Abbreviating Christmas to "Xmas" is seldom seen in printed media these days because grammarians frown on it as shoddy, and Christians may see it as irreverent if not profane. ("X" is an ancient and well-known symbol of Christ and the cross.)

The "eleventh hour," also a metaphor for the last minute, is an ancient expression as well. The term comes from a parable in the Gospel According to St. Matthew — that of a vineyard owner who hires workers at the beginning of a 12-hour day. He promises each a penny for the day's work. Throughout the day, even up to the eleventh hour, the owner hires more workers. And at the end of the day, he pays each a penny, whether the worker's day was short or long.

That parable is taken by Christians to represent the gift of grace. But it also offers one of our most familiar "time" expressions. We might hear, for example, that a prisoner condemned to death has received an eleventh-hour reprieve, meaning that his life was spared at the last minute.

Another running-out-of-time term is "last ditch," which is a battlefield's last line of defense. When we speak of a last-ditch effort, we mean that it's our final effort. The expression dates to the 1600s, when William of Orange said that rather than see his country's defeat, he would die alone in the last ditch.

"Under the wire" is another last-minute expression. It

comes from the racetrack, where the wire is a metaphor for the finish line. The first horse to get in *under the wire* wins the race.

So here we are — almost to the wire. I once read of an instructive bit of graffiti on a Dallas restroom wall — scrawled, apparently, by a public facility philosopher: "Time was invented to keep everything from happening at once." It may seem that there are too many things happening at the moment. But we can take comfort in the fact that however it seems, at least *everything* isn't happening.

Happy holidays!

PART FOUR

WORDS AND MEDIA

CHAPTER 34

FREAKY DEAKIES

When a Fox News reporter referred to "the horseless rider" during Ronald Reagan's funeral procession, I created a folder called "freaky deakies." It contains weird mistakes from the media, and if it were not a computer folder, we could accurately term it "bulging."

A sampling:

• A newspaper want ad for an office manager specified that the applicant must be "prophetic" in Microsoft Office.

• Pet advertisements often note that a dog or cat has

been "spaded," but you have to wonder if the following pet ad was even in the right section: "Datsun — free to good home."

• One newspaper reporter wrote of the problem of "intimate domain," another wrote of a "died in the wool" Baptist, and still another wrote that a new policy should "expediate" local government efforts to help Katrina's victims.

• A business columnist, in a wham-bam groaner, wrote glowingly of a professional who had reached the "pinochle" of success in his personal "Alger Hiss" story. This writer meant Horatio Alger, a 19th-century preacher of the gospel of success, celebrated for his rags-to-riches themes. Alger *Hiss* was a U.S. State Department official famously accused of being a communist and Soviet spy in 1948.

• An entertainment reporter likewise garbled meaning when he mourned actor Jerry Orbach with the words: "His loss is irreplaceable." Another said: "We'll miss not seeing him."

• After a tornado hit Fort Worth, Texas, a local radio reporter announced that 12 square blocks would be "condored" off in the downtown area.

• A Dallas-Fort Worth TV news anchor, describing a tribute to a local luminary, said that the speakers shared "antidotes" during the banquet. (How bad *was* that food?)

• An on-screen text behind a TV anchor bannered: "TROOP WITHDRAWL." ("Soldiers with a Southern accent?" asked the viewer who sent me this freaky deaky.)

Sometimes TV sports announcers get so excited they seem not to know what they're saying. A Fox Sports announcer said before a NASCAR Busch series race that the area was "compromised" of three cities, two states, and a whole lot of beauty. An ABC-TV announcer said the quarterback was "telegrafting" where he intended to throw the ball. Another TV announcer screamed during a wrestling match that a wrestler was acting like a man "repossessed."

Good freakies can come from anywhere. ACLU attorney Margaret Winter produced one when she said that a prisoner should not have been put into the general population section of Wichita Falls' James Allred Unit, one of Texas' roughest prisons. In that environment, she said, the prisoner was like "catnip to a pack of wolves."

• The one-time governor of New Mexico warned that a politically tricky situation would be like "opening a box of Pandoras."

• And there's the politician who said it didn't matter if the bill was passed after the beginning of the "physical" year; they'd just make it "radioactive."

So it's no surprise that some of the best freaky deakies in my folder come not from the press, but from a frequent subject: the president of the United States. We've heard George W. Bush say he knows that "human beings and fish can co-exist peacefully," and that "America needs a military where breast and brightest are proud to serve," and that it's hard work to "put food on your family." And we know about "nucular." But he paired that mispronunciation with another in Waco, Texas, when he said that one of the goals was to reduce our "nucular" arsenal to a level "commisurate with" . . . whatever.

CHAPTER 35

PROFESSIONAL GAFFES

A story in a recent issue of *Quill* magazine bore this headline: "Editors: Spend time with enthused writers."

What's wrong with that?

The headline should read "*enthusiastic* writers." *Enthused* is a verb, not an adjective; the adjective is *enthusiastic*. (The *enthusiastic* writers *enthused* that the workshop had renewed their *enthusiasm*.) *Enthused*, a back formation of the noun *enthusiasm*, is still seen by many as colloquial, but colloquial or not, the word is not an adjective and is therefore incorrectly used in the above headline.

Is this worth mentioning? It is. Not just because it's incorrect, but because of the content and audience of this magazine — written by and for professional wordsmiths. This column has discussed the need for linguistic precision from professional communicators too many times to belabor the point here. Suffice it to say that we expect certain expertise from professionals of any stripe — doctor, lawyer, educator — and journalists are not exempt. Expertise means both depth of knowledge and proficient use of tools — and wordsmiths have only one tool: the word.

Maybe that's why we're surprised by misuse and malapropisms from writers, reporters, editors, and the like. From them, we expect accuracy and precision and are disappointed when those qualities are lacking.

Case in point: Here's an e-mail from an editor who compliments my work for, in part, its "notoriety." My work is *notorious*? (No jokes, please!) *Notorious* is confused with being of note, but it's pejorative, not complimentary: That actress is *noted* for her acting skill but *notorious* for her tantrums.

Recently, a newspaper reporter covered a speech I gave on writing — during which I said that we sometimes fear the clarity of simplicity, either because of timidity or because of blindly emulating the wrong writers.

Here's what the reporter wrote — or, in any case, what was published:

"Ms. LaRocque spoke of the 'fear of simplicity, which sometimes comes from timidity or from blindly immolating the wrong people.' "

Of course I laughed when I read it, just as you're laughing now. *Immolate* means to sacrifice, or to kill as a sacrifice. Because sacrifice often involves burning, we might hear "self-immolation" regarding the practice of setting oneself afire — in other words, sacrificing oneself, often as a protest.

So "*immolating* the wrong people" — interesting as that concept is — came nowhere near the intended meaning of *imitating* the wrong people. Confusing *immolate* and *emulate* creates such odd effects that one hopes the reader divines the real intent. Still, the reporter's passage above is a direct quotation, not a paraphrase, which may leave the reader wondering: *Who doesn't know the differ-*

ence between "immolate" and "emulate" — the speaker or the reporter and the reporter's editors?

That reporter and her editors may not have known the meaning of *immolate*, but at least they used a real word — something the following reporter did not: "Police say she was killed because of Ms. Barry's *infuriation* over a flirtation between her and Ms. Barry's fiancé." Here, the writer ignores the noun *fury* and creates a new noun from the verb *infuriate*.

A TV reporter created an odd hybrid when he spoke of the out-of-control vehicle as having *vareened* around a curve. That coinage is presumably a blend of *careened* and *veered*.

Like "infuriation," mistakes in word use sometimes make a weird sort of sense. For example, a radio reporter mentioned "the *rigamaroar*" surrounding a certain issue — rather than the correct *rigmarole*. The "roar" in the created word "rigamaroar" at least suggested the reporter's meaning.

Another such mistake is calling a *manila folder* a "vanilla folder," which perhaps refers to the folder's color. "Manila" refers to the kind of paper such folders are made of, however.

While some wrong words can make sense, they more often distort meaning, as in this gaffe from an entertainment reporter: "She knew the director and *wrangled* an invitation to audition for the movie." This context (she knew the director, therefore . . .) shows that the writer meant *wangle*. *Wrangle* means to quarrel, squabble, or bicker — or, in an entirely different context, something cowboys do. *Wangle*, however, means to get or arrange through contrivance or finagling, which was the context of this statement.

Speaking of *bicker*, as we were in defining *wrangle*, an editor said she'd bought a car after hours of *bickering* with the dealers. She probably meant *dickering*, which means to bargain, barter, or haggle, and which is what you do if you're trying to get a lower price or better deal. *Bickering*, which means to squabble, would hardly gain the desired result.

Many people misunderstand and misuse words from time to time, but professional wordsmiths hope to do it the least. And those who do it the least are those who read the most. Heavy readers usually have not only the largest but also the most precise and accurate vocabularies. That's because seeing words at work, in their contexts, is the best way to avoid confusion. Those who have seen *emulate*, *rigmarole*, *manila folder*, or *wangle* on a page are less likely to blunder in their use or to confuse them with similar words.

Aside from the confusion and embarrassment using words incorrectly can bring to professional communicators, it also sends a valuable reminder: Those who *can* read, but do not, have no advantage over those who *cannot* read. And if we haven't spent a lifetime reading? Then we need at least one good reference work on usage. Bookstore and library shelves offer plenty of choices; get the one that best suits your needs.

CHAPTER 36

MIXAPHORS

Media communicators often use colorful figures of speech to make their words livelier or more human and conversational. That device can work — provided the figure of speech isn't trite and provided the communicator actually knows the expression. Misunderstanding figures of speech leads to "mixaphors" or otherwise mangled expression.

For example, an editor on a panel said that unless all aspects of a procedure were carefully controlled, things could go "hog-wired" — an imaginative but meaningless blend of "haywire," "hog wild" and, possibly, "hog-tied."

A TV anchor said he was so sick with the flu that he felt he had "one foot in the bucket" — apparently blending "one foot in the grave" with "kick the bucket."

A radio commentator said that one problem in the Middle East was that there was no roadmap at the end of the tunnel. That mixaphor made some sense and could have passed for word play — after all, we'd like not only light at the end of the tunnel but also to know where we're going.

That commentator lost all credibility, however, when he went on to mention the "grindstone" around negotiators' necks. If we'd listened longer, he might have had someone's nose to the millstone, or even to the albatross.

For the record: We wear a millstone or albatross around our necks and put our noses to the grindstone. Millstones, symbolizing a heavy burden, are large stones that pulverize (as in processing grain). A grindstone is a revolving stone that hones or polishes, so we put our noses to the grindstone, figuratively speaking, when we work hard. And the albatross around our necks symbolizes a burden that hinders action.

While mixaphors lose their original sense through combination, some expressions are abbreviated over time — although the shorthand version may not make sense. For example, the expression that began as "happy as a clam at high tide" is now simply — and less meaningfully — "happy as a clam."

How happy *are* clams, exactly?

"Walking on eggs," which meant stepping carefully to avoid breaking those fragile shells, has become "walking on eggshells." But if the eggs are already broken, why not just stomp away — the damage is done.

Expressions also can change over time through misuse. As word guru William Safire observed regarding usage and misusage: *When enough of us are wrong, we're right.*

The expression "running amok," for example, is sometimes rendered "amuck." The term, meaning out of control, derives from the Malayan word *amoq*, which described people in a frenzy. *Amok* is so frequently misspelled, though, that some dictionaries list "amuck" as an alternative (if not preferred) form.

An editor at a writers' conference made the audience jittery when he said his computer system was "jury-rigged." Those writers knew he meant "jerry-rigged" or "jerry-built."

That expression is especially interesting, however, because "jury-rigged," which we now see as incorrect, was in fact the original term. "Jerry-built" refers to anything hastily and haphazardly constructed, and while there's controversy concerning its origin, its most plausible derivation is nautical. Old-time sailors once replaced broken masts with flimsy temporary poles that often fell on crew members and came to be called "injury masts." In time, "injury" was shortened to "jury," and "jury mast" was followed by the terms "jury-built" or "jury-rigged." Jury was promptly slurred to "jerry" — a serendipitous development because the later term "rigging a jury" has an entirely different meaning and history.

An e-mail from a journalist includes the solecism: "hanging by tenderhooks." That's a baffling construction — what would a "tender hook" be like? Granted, *tenterhook* isn't entirely suggestive, either. But a tenterhook is a sharp, hooked nail used to fasten cloth to a . . . yes, to a *tenter* — which in turn is used to dry and stretch cloth.

So if you're on tenterhooks, metaphorically, you're stretched, strained, suspended.

I wonder: When those sharp, hooked nails become dull, do we put our tenterhooks to the grindstone?

CHAPTER 37

WRONG WORDS

When we marked the anniversary of Sept. 11, 2001, we also marked a year of media misuse of the word "anniversary."

In the 12 months that followed the destruction of the World Trade Center, we heard and read about that day's one-month, three-month, and six-month "anniversaries," but Sept. 11, 2002, was the first real anniversary. That's because "anniversary" means the *yearly recurrence of the date of a past event*. Nothing under a year can be an anniversary. The root of "anni" means "year," and the root of "versary" means "to turn" — literally, the turning of a year.

Many words derive from the same "annus" root. Thus, *annual* means of or measured by a year (as in annual salary), or occurring once a year (as in event or publication). An *annal* is a written account of events arranged chronologically year by year. The *annual ring* seen in a cross-section of a tree trunk represents a year's growth.

Since *anni* means "year," it's redundant to say one-year, or 10-year, or 50-year anniversary — the graceful way to express it is *first, 10th,* or *50th anniversary.*

Most usage problems come from mimicry — from borrowing words we don't understand from others who don't understand. And a hazy understanding of what words mean is particularly troublesome for professional communicators. Consider the following:

- A television news anchor: "He's a novitiate when it comes to inside-the-beltway politics." This anchor meant *novice*. A *novitiate* is a place, not a person; it's where novices stay.

- A political commentator: "This so-called reform bill flaunts the Constitution." He means *flout*, and because he doesn't understand his own words, he confuses both his meaning and his readers. *Flaunt* means to show off or display; *flout* means to scorn or treat with disdain.

- An editor: "I'm a big fan of the nut graf. I find it's a good device for honing in on the key point of a story." It's worrisome that this copy editor doesn't know the difference between *home* in and *hone*. "Hone" means to sharpen, and "home in" is what homing pigeons do — that is, they go home; they aim for the mark. A missile homes in on the target; a barber hones his razor.

- A reporter: "What did they put in his coffee, and more importantly, where can I get some?" Another reporter: "Most importantly, these precautions help to lower your risk of developing skin cancer." *Most important* is the correct expression. The words are an elliptical expression for "what is more important," so writing "more importantly" is like writing "what is more importantly."

- A political writer: "The correspondence between Kenneth Lay and the governor's office ran the gambit from personal thank-you notes to forceful lobbying." She means *gamut*, a range or scale. A *gambit* is a maneuver or ploy, as in the opening gambit in a chess game.

• A police reporter refers to the "vagaries" of a witness' account. The reporter probably is confusing "vagary" with "vagueness," but the word has nothing to do with vagueness, obscurity, or uncertainty. A *vagary* is an odd, capricious, unpredictable, or whimsical action or idea.

• A reporter: "The voters said they were reticent to support a provision they didn't understand." Confusing *reticent* with *reluctant* is a major usage problem in the media. *Reticent* means to be taciturn, quiet, reluctant to speak — it does not mean to be reluctant to do anything else. In the passage above, those voters were reluctant to support the provision, but they obviously weren't reticent about it.

• "Begs the question" is also widely misused by media writers. "Begs the question" does not mean "raise the question." It means to use a circular argument that assumes as proved the very point you're trying to prove. We'd be begging the question, for example, if we claimed that parallel lines would never meet, and offered as proof the fact that the lines were parallel. Or we'd be begging the question if we supported a claim that scripture was inspired because scripture says it is.

Failing to understand a word or expression and therefore using it incorrectly is one sort of communication problem. But sometimes we annoy our audience by creating ugly new words where attractive old ones already exist. The habit of adding "ness" to a word willy-nilly is such a practice. I recently read the coinage "unpreciseness," for example, rather than *imprecision*. We often read in the sports pages about an athlete's "ineptness," when the perfectly good noun for this meaning is *ineptitude*. A direct quotation in a recent news story contained the word "cumbersomeness," when *cumbersome* says it. Reporters shouldn't change direct quotes, of course, but they can always paraphrase.

In short, when we search for "accurateness," "clearness," "readableness," and "briefness," we should seek instead *accuracy, clarity, readability*, and *brevity*.

CHAPTER 38

MEDIA MISTAKES
HURT THE LANGUAGE

One consequence of an influential mass media is its attendant influence on the language. If media speakers and writers are wordsmiths whose expression is precise and graceful, the impact on the language will be positive. If not, that impact will be negative. People are influenced by what they read, and excellence in communication is always threatened by the inaccurate, illogical, or banal.

Consider the following examples from various media:

• *Newspaper headline:* "Malvo takes credit for several shootings."

That headline should read "takes *blame.*" We receive "credit" for laudable acts, and the sniper murders were hardly laudable.

• *Radio*: The reporter, whose story concerned a man who'd shot a doctor who performed abortions, said that the shooter had admitted feeling *badly* that the doctor died. "Feel badly" is a common but nevertheless basic mistake — one professional communicators shouldn't make. We use adjectives, not adverbs, with sense or linking verbs, and *feel* is, of course, a sense verb. We feel bad or stupid or hungry or angry. We don't feel badly, stupidly, hungrily, or angrily any more than we *seem* badly, stupidly, hungrily, or angrily. Imagine these lyrics: "I feel prettily, oh so prettily, I feel prettily and wittily and brightly."

• *Television*: "Only gold is one of the best ways" to protect your investment dollar. Here's a business reporter who doesn't know what *only* means. Nothing can be *the only way* at the same time that it is *one of the ways*. This speaker would have to say either "Gold is the only way," "Gold is the best way," or "Gold is one of the better ways."

The word "only" frequently causes trouble. "One of the only," for example, is a bewildering and nonsensical phrase we've already discussed. *Only* also is often misplaced: "She only gave up hard liquor" can also mean "Only she gave up hard liquor." The proper placement of *only* avoids confusion: "She gave up only hard liquor."

• *Newspaper:* "As the president offered his lofty 'vision thing' for spawning democracy in the Middle East, America was at a rough juncture. The administration opened a can of worms in Iraq."

In that hackneyed passage, we have the worn "lofty vision," the stale "rough juncture," the overworked "spawned," and — as if that weren't enough — a can of worms.

Why not the can of beans as well?

Here's more overheated newspaper writing:

• "The Bush crowd hurtled into Baghdad on the law of Disney: Wishing can make it so. Now they're ensnared in the law of the jungle: the rules of engagement don't apply with this scary cocktail of Saddam loyalists, foreign fighters and terrorists, who hold nothing sacred, not human rights organizations, humanitarian groups or Iraqi civilians."

Count 'em: *Wishing makes it so, law of the jungle, rules of engagement, scary cocktail, hold nothing sacred*. A pile of platitudes yields writing as corny as it is clichéd.

• *Newspaper:* A story on airline fares asks: "Need to find out which seats are *currently* available for a particular flight?" No, we'd like to know which seats were available last week. Words such as *currently* and *now* are often obvious, if not ridiculous.

• *Radio*: A talk show host, discussing whether Shakespeare's early acting career helped him as a playwright, said: "You couldn't scratch an actor in the western world who wouldn't say so."

That statement is an odd distortion of the expression *scratch [something], find [something]* — for example, scratch a politician, find a liar. It means that when you scratch the surface of something or someone, you find something or someone else beneath. If the speaker had said, "Scratch an actor, find a playwright," listeners would understand the implication. But as rendered, the statement is as meaningless as it is weird.

• *Television:* The anchor said, "The chopper was *completely destroyed,* except for its tail section." *Completely destroyed* is redundant — d*estroyed* means ruined or demolished, so the sense of "completely" is built into the word. The redundancy is doubly awkward here because of the phrase "except for its tail section." Obviously, it *wasn't* "completely" destroyed.

• *Newspaper:* "The barge *sunk* immediately after the incident." Back to grammar school. *Sank.*

• *Radio:* "Witnesses said he had been drinking before

he *dove* into the shallow end of the pool." Grammar school again. *Dived*.

• *Television:* "She *creeped* back into the room after the awards ceremony." Grammar school is getting crowded. *Crept*.

Basic errors such as those we saw above are common, yes, but they should not appear in the work of professional wordsmiths. They embarrass the media daily, and their effect on everyone and everything is negative. First, they damage the credibility of writer, editor, speaker, and medium alike. Second, they foster bad language habits and add to the general burden of shoddy and careless expression.

As one annoyed reader put it: "Pay attention to the media, and you don't know *what's* right anymore!"

CHAPTER 39

BEAT JARGON

For journalists, one of the greatest hazards in covering a beat is beat jargon, which can shut out the average reader. And the longer a reporter covers a certain beat, the greater the hazard. That's because the more we hear certain words and expressions, the more they sound like . . . well, like *English*.

Beat writers are well advised to return to a time when they didn't know the jargon of their beats. They probably felt inadequate for the not knowing, but their lack of insider knowledge was in a sense the reader's ally. Good reporters either omit or translate the unclear, and they're better able to do that if they know which terms are potential stumbling blocks to understanding. Unhappily, reporters sometimes become seduced by the jargon of their beats and begin to use it themselves. But it doesn't help the reader if the writer "goes native."

Revisiting one's "ignorance" in no way diminishes the necessity of thoroughly learning one's beat — and that includes its language. Only through full understanding can we accurately reflect a beat's complexity and nuance.

Nor does translating jargon into common terms in any way "dumb down" the message — it merely makes the work accessible to the lay reader at first reading.

Sometimes writers balk, though — in part because they want to show off their knowledge. But trotting out an arcane or specialized vocabulary doesn't demonstrate knowledge. Rather, one test of genius is the ability to couch the complex in simple terms.

As Einstein said: "Everything should be as simple as possible — but no simpler."

Good communicators who cover, say, the medical beat know that the prefix "therm-" means heat or temperature, but they write "sunstroke," not *thermoplegia* — even if their expert source uses the latter term. Likewise, good reporters may know that the suffix "-algia" means pain, and "-rhea" means flow. But they write "toothache," not *dentalgia*. And "runny nose," not *rhinorrhea*.

These days, beat reporters often have degrees in the topics they cover. So a reporter who went to law school, say, covers law. Such education and background is a decided advantage for certain beats.

But if the lawyer journalist uses the same language in his or her stories as his lawyer source, this marriage of like to like is hardly a consummation devoutly to be wished. How much *per curiam* (by the court), *actus reus* (criminal act), and *ab initio* (from the beginning) can readers take?

Beats such as medicine, law, or education aren't the only ones that present the challenges of jargon. The business world is cluttered with all manner of jargon and, like the military beat, is clotted with acronyms that mean little or nothing to the average reader. Most readers probably know, for example, that CEO, R&D, MBO, and SOP mean chief executive officer, research and development, management by objective, and standard operating procedure.

But equally common — and less known — are ZBB (zero-based budgeting), AQL (acceptable quality level), and PERT (performance evaluation and review technique).

Business generates so many acronyms that reporters covering that beat have to be careful or their stories will not only be unclear, they will also look like alphabet soup.

Even such beats as automotive, real estate, and fashion are laden with jargon. Cover cars a while, and you'll learn that "postignition" means the engine that continues to run after it's turned off. Or that the "dwell meter" measures the "dwell angle" of the distributor points. But try telling that to the average reader.

Covering the world of Realtors and real estate can be almost as incomprehensible as covering medicine or law. Readers plowing though untranslated jargon such as "incorporeal realty" (intangible elements or nonmaterial rights of a property), "escalator clause" (a feature in some mortgages or leases allowing increases in terms or rents), or "appurtenances" (rights, benefits, or possessions additional to the actual property purchase).

And fashion? You're drunk on jargon the moment you step into the Garment District. Yes, Seventh Avenue, Carnaby Street — where the rag trade thrives. But do we *all* know that, and will the story suffer if we don't?

Are we safe in entertainment, at least? Or in sports and recreation? Those aren't technical beats, and the readers are personally involved in the beat's activities, so wouldn't they know more of the beat jargon?

I guess most of us understand soaps and shoots and sweeps and spinoffs by now. But "Thirty Rock"? When did that become NBC-TV headquarters (30 Rockefeller

Plaza) and who knew?

We haven't even mentioned the police beat, an often nonnegotiable terrain of unnecessary jargon. I mean! *The perpetrator exited the vehicle and fled on foot.*

But don't get me started.

CHAPTER 40

GOOD BROADCASTING
IS GOOD DIALOGUE

Two annoying practices in broadcast news presentation are supposedly off-the-cuff dialogue that sounds as if it's being read, and speech jammed with journalese. Both problems can occur any time but are typical when anchors question reporters or press them for further detail — a practice designed to produce an informal discussion of the news.

In the first case — supposedly impromptu remarks that seem read — the reporter sounds rehearsed. Viewers and listeners are made uncomfortable when what is offered as spontaneous seems scripted or artificial. Knowing that, reporters often begin their remarks with conversational hitches such as "well" or "um" in an effort to seem more natural. But then their words flow freely and seamlessly in the distinctive "reading aloud" monotone.

It's a small matter, agreed, but nevertheless important because it also seems a small sham.

Of course, it's good to plan our words, even to speak from notes. But presenting a written text as though it were speech takes special skill. The best defense against sounding as though we're reading is to use in our notes only keywords — not complete sentences. Keywords remind us of what we want to say, but force us to formulate coherent statements about the subject. Complete sentences, on the other hand, tempt us to turn off thought and simply read.

Another defense against the reading aloud hazard is to speak from knowledge. Reporters who know their story very well and who have a logical sequence of keywords in their notes speak more forcefully, imaginatively, and engagingly.

Once we can speak naturally on the air, we should turn our attention to our vocabulary. Both print and broadcast journalists face the problem of clichéd or hackneyed expression, but the problem is most acute for those who speak rather than write. They haven't the luxury of a rough draft.

When anchors question reporters or press them for further detail, reporters have a rare chance to show personality and polish in their responses. But that situation also lays bare the vocabulary. Is it fresh or stale? Original or trite? Extemporaneous speech immediately exposes dependence upon journalese, the language of hacks.

It's in unscripted speaking that we're most likely to hear journalism's stock expressions — threadbare nouns such as *defining moment, worst-case scenario, cautiously optimistic, firestorm of criticism, heated debate, stunning victory, staggering defeat, chilling effect, ground swell, surprise move, bizarre twist, litany, laundry list.*

Adjectives are equally stale: *unprecedented, burgeoning, beleaguered, embattled.* And so are verbs: *spawn, spark, spur, trigger, target, decimate, escalate, spiral, launch, unleash, resonate.*

One of the most overused expressions in broadcast news is getting or having a "sense of." Consider this exchange between an anchor and reporter:

"Is it your sense that the legislators' outrage is genuine? I mean, that they had no . . . no, uh, sense that this spying was going on domestically?"

"No. I mean, yes. That's my, uh, sense."

We can hear that anchor struggling to find the word "idea," rather than repeat the less meaningful word "sense." But she fails. Likewise, we can hear the reporter's discomfort with repeating yet again the word "sense."

Dictionaries provide us with the meaning of the noun "sense" for such a context: a feeling, impression, or perception through the senses, as in a sense of warmth; or a generalized feeling, awareness, or realization, such as a sense of longing. So, getting a "sense of" is a flawed choice for contexts that demand concreteness or refer to factual, tangible matters such as numbers or amounts.

Despite that, we hear broadcast journalists asking: "Do you have any sense of how many were hurt or killed?" "Did you get a sense of how much this program would cost?" "Can you give us a sense of how the administration might react?"

Could the questions be more gracefully and credibly put? Yes. *Do you know? Did they say how much? How might the administration react?* Each of those questions has answers, and we don't have to rely on our senses to find them: *yes* or *no; they don't know; the administration could react several ways.*

Are there successful "sense of" constructions? Sure. Here's one: "When interviewing the candidates, did you get a sense of hostility or distrust?" Here the abstract "did you get a sense of" is useful: We're asking the reporter if he could "read" the candidates' unspoken attitudes through his senses. It's a valuable and aptly put question that could yield an interesting and insightful answer.

But we should reserve this overused expression for situations in which it best applies. Throughout history, the memorable and credible communicator has chosen plain talk over faddish terms. So should journalists, both print and broadcast.

CHAPTER 41

REFUGEE: WORDS AS MESSAGE RATHER THAN MEDIUM

One apparent "victim" in Hurricane Katrina's aftermath is the word *refugee*. The word is embroiled in controversy, with some saying it's a racist term that identifies Katrina's victims as second-class citizens and perhaps as not even Americans.

The Rev. Jesse Jackson and the members of the Congressional Black Caucus have said so, and President Bush echoed on Sept. 6: "The people we're talking about are not refugees. They are Americans, and they need the help and love and compassion of our fellow citizens."

The controversy has caused some news organizations — among them *The Washington Post, The Miami Herald* and *The Boston Globe* — to ban *refugee* in their Katrina coverage. The Associated Press and *The New York Times* continue to use the word where they think appropriate.

Is *refugee* guilty as charged? No. But that's beside the point.

The term was first applied to the French Huguenots who fled to England after the revocation of the Edict of Nantes in 1685. Traditionally, a refugee has been one who seeks refuge in a foreign country because of war or political or religious persecution. That's how the Oxford English Dictionary defines it, and that's probably what the word calls to mind for most people. But Webster's New World Dictionary defines it more broadly as "a person who flees from home or country to seek refuge elsewhere, as in a time of war or of political or religious persecution."

The AP reported that NYT wordsmith William Safire said he did not see how *refugee* had any racial implications, that a refugee is a person who seeks refuge and can be of any race. Mr. Safire added, however, that he would probably simply use "flood victims" to avoid any political connotations that *refugee* may have assumed in this debate.

That seems the wise course. Words must mean, finally, what the majority think they mean, and whatever a word's "real" meaning, if people think it is hurtful, then it is hurtful to them. If they think it's an insult, then it is insulting to them.

And in practical terms, even if *refugee* is not racist, it's still probably less than precise in some cases — because of its broadening definition. We have any number of untainted and uncontested words to describe Katrina's sufferers. Those who were evacuated are "victims" and "evacuees"; those who fled earlier on their own are "victims" and "survivors"; most of the victims are "displaced" or "those who sought refuge."

The point is that if *refugee* is offensive for any reason, real or imagined, it gets in the way of the message.

Words matter, yes. But perception matters, too. When a word acquires a taint, with or without justification, it obscures the message. People start thinking about the word and its intent, rather than the message's content. In other words, they think about the medium rather than the message. When a word is stained by a charge of any "ism," it's time to give it a rest and let it recover if it can. It has acquired emotional baggage and will sully otherwise clear and effective communication.

Some might say that's bowing to the excesses of political correctness, but there's always a way to communicate meaningfully, accurately, and without offense. Our language has more than 600,000 words and is rich in synonym and near-synonym.

A final point. That we're discussing this at all at such a critical time shows how much words matter. But thousands of Americans are dead and dying and displaced. Of all Katrina's innocent victims, this little word is the least of them. It will survive, as perhaps many human beings did not, and focusing on its meaning or use is a distraction that trivializes such monumental tragedy.

Chapter 42

The Victim as Media Scapegoat

Nothing engenders more distrust of the media than careless or hurtful treatment of victims. Yet, despite all good intentions, further victimizing the victim does happen in news stories. Consider the bare bones of this story, which appeared in two metropolitan dailies on the same morning (principal names are changed; all else is the same):

Billy Ryan, 17, and friend Josh Cook were outside Josh's house about 4 a.m. when they saw a man breaking into a neighbor's car. The boys called 911 and confronted the man, who scuffled with Billy and then stabbed him to death. The man and his companion fled in the companion's car but were arrested later and held without bail on charges of murder while committing a felony.

Newspaper One's story begins with those salient facts, then adds:

But beyond that, details are sketchy. Police said one of the teens had a gun with him, but they are unsure which teen had it or how he came to possess it. Officials are also uncertain why the teens were out at 4 a.m. . . .

Veronica Clay, a spokeswoman for Smithville

Independent School District, said that the victim never showed up at Venture High School in January. The teen entered the alternative school in October after leaving Polk High School.

The story ends there. Earlier, it also mentions that a friend said Billy "bounced around a lot."

Consider the subtle but negative impact of the words *uncertain why the teens were out at 4 a.m., never showed up at Venture High School, bounced around a lot.* The story in Newspaper One leaves readers with this impression: Some kid, a high-school no-show who "bounced around a lot" (whatever that means) and may have had a gun, was out at 4 a.m. and was stabbed to death in a street fight.

How did the victim come to be the goat? After all, he died trying to stop a robbery. Newspaper One gives more space to careless, incomplete, and ultimately inaccurate allusion about the victim than it gives to facts about the killer — who, we learn from the other newspaper, has been arrested several times, both for burglary and for aggravated assault with a deadly weapon. Those facts are not mentioned in Newspaper One's story.

Newspaper Two's story, however — which begins with the same bare bones presented in the second paragraph above — adds that the boys were sitting in a pickup in front of Josh's house when they saw the man breaking into the car:

Ryan was spending the night at Cook's house, and the two were outside smoking cigarettes, according to Cook's mother, Doris, who said she would not allow them to smoke in the house . . . .

Monday evening, Ryan's friends gathered to remember

him, said Doris Cook.

'We're still in shock,' she said. 'One moment he's here; the next he's gone.'

Doris Cook said that Billy and Josh knew each other from Polk High School. She described him as a good person who loved his mother.

'He was always respectful toward adults,' Cook said. 'You could tell that he was a nice person just by being around him.'

We then hear from the same spokeswoman quoted in Newspaper One's story, Veronica Clay. Here, she says that after leaving Polk High, Billy Ryan attended the alternative school Venture High, which, among other things, was geared toward dropouts who have returned to finish their education. The story continues: Ryan dropped out of Venture on Jan. 20 and said he was going to pursue his GED, Clay said.

Sounds like a different story in some important ways, doesn't it? (A follow-up story in Newspaper Two said it was in fact Cook who had the gun and scuffled with the man and that Billy Ryan was stabbed when he tried to defend his friend. That story also said that Billy had arranged for a GED program and would then work at his uncle's masonry company.)

Newspaper Two not only presents a more fully reported version of the story — answering questions left unanswered by the story in Newspaper One — but it also presents a fuller, fairer profile of Billy Ryan. In Newspaper One, he seems a juvenile throwaway: never showed up at school, nobody knew why he was out at 4 a.m., bounced around a lot . . . .

And let's say all that is true. Should he be murdered? Should we care less? More important, is it relevant to this story? Is irresponsible and harsh treatment of victims just another way of blaming the victim? Ah, she would never have been raped if she hadn't worn those short skirts. If he hadn't gone into that sleazy bar . . . .

In Newspaper Two, Billy Ryan might well be a boy with problems, but people care about him as a nice kid who had plans and "loved his mother." What must it be like for that mother, who in her grief must also deal with news stories that paint her slain son as an unsupervised dropout, somebody who maybe *didn't matter that much*?

Fair and balanced treatment of victims has nothing to do with slanting stories, distorting or omitting fact, or with sentimentalism or mawkishness or even advocacy. But it does have to do with human decency. Sometimes, to be sure, even the most ethical journalism hurts innocent people. But ethical journalism is also quick to distinguish between the hurtful but relevant and necessary, and the irrelevant, irresponsible, or unfair.

PART FIVE

WORDS AND MECHANICS

CHAPTER 43

DEPARTMENT OF REDUNDANCY DEPARMENT

I can't be the only one who's noticed the shoddy editing not only in newspapers and magazines, but also in books — even in textbooks and best-sellers. Let's make that *especially* in best-sellers. Some authors are headed for best-sellerdom no matter how they write, so their publishers apparently give editing a short shrift. They'll make money anyway.

Typos abound in books, even those from large and reputable publishing houses. So do errors in grammar, structure, punctuation and usage. One mega-seller author wrote, for example, that a character "cavorted" in her deck chair. What can we make of a "wordsmith" who doesn't know that you must at least get out of your chair to cavort? And even if the professional writer doesn't know, shouldn't the professional editor? It's not unreasonable to expect wordsmiths to know their way around the world of words — after all, the word is their only tool.

Grammar and structure problems can be complex and challenging, but what excuses the gross redundancies littering many books? How much skill does it take to know better than to write "free gift"? Characters in novels "shrug their shoulders" or "nod their heads," when the least discerning wordsmith knows there's nothing else to shrug or nod. I recently read of "continuous, nonstop terrorist threats." But "continuous" means "nonstop" — does saying it twice make the threats any more ceaseless? Such redundancy is as blind to what words mean as "completely decapitated" or "totally demolished."

Most of us commit redundancies in speech and should be forgiven. But writing offers a wonderful luxury: We can review and rewrite — endlessly, if we like — before dusting our hands and declaring the work as proficient as our talents will allow.

In editing, writers commune with themselves, and the questions involving redundancies are basic: Hmm, added bonus, eh? Isn't a bonus always additional and therefore always "added"? And what's with "12 noon" and "12 midnight" and "10 a.m. in the morning"? Shouldn't that be noon, midnight, 10 a.m.?

It's easy to spot redundancies such as *end result, sum*

total, true fact, basic fundamental, consensus of opinion, potential promise, exact same, repeat again, personal friend, round in shape, blue in color, past experience, refer back to, advance warning. And a bit of thoughtful editing unearths subtler gaffes — "foreign imports," say, instead of *imports.* (All imports are foreign.) Or "hot-water heater" instead of *water heater.* (Why heat it if it's already hot?)

Some redundancies are overlooked because they've sneaked into the vernacular. "PIN number," for example. "PIN" means personal identification number, so "PIN number" means "personal identification number number." Ditto "ATM machine," which means "automated teller machine machine." Ditto "HIV virus," which means "human immunodeficiency virus virus."

A holder of a doctoral degree referred to it as a "doctorate degree," a redundancy because a doctorate *is* a degree.

The word *new* is often redundant. The military refers to "new recruits," but aren't they all? When they're no longer new, aren't they also no longer recruits?

Sportswriters refer to "setting a *new* record," but, again, *all* records are new. How would you set an *old* record?

Business publications refer to "new innovations" and "new initiatives." But what would it be like to come up with *old* innovations and *old* initiatives?

Many redundancies are as illogical as they are repetitive. An acquaintance said, for example, that she hoped to get a "temporary loan." But loans that aren't temporary aren't loans at all. They're gifts.

Bet they're not *free* gifts.

It's not only redundant to join words that have the same meaning, it's also flabby and unrefined — and unnecessarily so in writing, where we have that rare chance to second-guess the way we express ourselves.

Chapter 44

Weird Quotation Marks

Ever since I saw a mailbox bearing the legend *The "Smiths,"* I've noticed errant quotation marks everywhere. They're not just surrounding, as we would expect, dialogue or direct quotations:

"Hey," he said.

"Hey, yourself," she responded.

Nor are the errant quotation marks surrounding, say, a nickname: Tony "The Fink" Ratzo. Or a figure of speech: Forget biology — the "psychological clock" ticks even louder. Or an ironic turn of phrase or contradiction: Hey, those are "groovy" purple plaid pants ya got there, guy.

Nor are quotation marks confined to other clear and predictable uses: certain titles, for example, or brief passages of prose or poetry. The crazy quotation marks are just *there*, doing no discernible task except confusing or amusing — particularly because we use quotation marks in part to signal the reader: *Not really!*

Increasingly, it seems that quotation marks are added for emphasis. But they don't work that way. We have ways of adding emphasis — italics, capital letters, boldfaced type, underlines, exclamation points — but the quotation mark isn't one of them. Yet, here's an ad for a "new" house; what are we to make of that? Is it irony? Is that house really new? Or is it, in fact, not so new? The same ad refers to the home's spacious "living" area. If not *really* for the living, what kind of home is this? A funeral home?

And consider this sign in a strip mall window: *We "dry clean" your finest apparel for a fraction of the cost.* Hmm. So what's going on here — they stick our finest apparel in the Maytag, add some detergent, hit "cold"? No wonder it costs less.

An ad for a special shampoo claims to make *color-treated hair completely "natural-looking."* What more can they do, exactly, to my "color-treated" hair? I mean, it already doesn't look "natural."

A supermarket in Dallas not only advertises *Krab Legs*, but surrounds that concoction with quotation marks. What might "krab" legs be? An imitation of a fake?

A label on a jewelry cleaner says it *preserves and protects your "precious" jewelry.* They must have sneaked a peek at my "jewels." Speaking of jewels, I once saw a small placard in a hotel room advising the occupant: *Please feel free to leave your valuables at the desk, or use the "safe" in your room.* Those quotation marks make that "safe" seem anything but.

There's no shortage of quotation mark oddities. Here are a few more:

• A sign in a bakery: *Our cakes are made with "real" coconut.* (Yum, wood shavings.)

• A menu item: *Sizzling "pork" patties.* (Where's Fido?)

• A menu note: *All our recipes are made with the finest "olive oil."* (Lard, right?)

• A newspaper ad: *Call now and ask to talk to one of*

our "friendly" telephone operators. (Ask for Grouchy Gertie or Crabby Carrie.)

- On the back of a CD: *Recorded "live" at the Tivoli Concert Hall.* (A moribund performance.)

- A freeway sign in Houston: *Road "Work" Ahead.* (Truth in advertising.)

- An ad for an eyeglass clinic: *Tired of those lines in your lenses? Ask to see our graduated "thin" lenses.* (You can also use these lenses to set ants on fire.)

- Company ad: *When you call us, you'll speak to a "human" being.* (Cheetah, will you get that phone?)

- A sign at a craft show: *Genuine "leather" belts.* (Genuine vinyl, no?)

- A sign on a roadside stand: *"Fresh" fruit.* (Beware the word "fresh" in quotation marks.)

- A carnival booth sign: *"Free!" 30-minute session with "Madame Xavier," our "psychic."* (Real name: Hortense Oglethorpe, and if she were *really* psychic, she'd warn you to beware the word "free" in quotation marks.)

- A clinic sign: *Free "Flu" shots.* (Whatever those shots are really for, at least they're really free.)

- Another clinic sign: *Free breast "examinations."* (Hmm, wonder what they're doing in there. Good thing they're not charging.)

Back to that mailbox bearing the label *The "Smiths."* Makes you wonder who *really* lives there. Maybe someone in the Witness Protection Program. Maybe Tony "The Fink" Ratzo. Oops. I mean Tony The Fink "Smith."

CHAPTER 45

APOSTROPHES

The success of Lynne Truss' *Eats, Shoots and Leaves* — a book on punctuation — is doubtless due in part to the amusing gag that gives the book its title:

A panda walks into a café. He orders a sandwich, eats it, then draws a gun and fires two shots in the air.

'Why,' asks the confused waiter, as the panda makes toward the exit. The panda produces a badly punctuated wildlife manual and tosses it over his shoulder.

'I'm a panda,' he says, at the door. 'Look it up.'

The waiter turns to the relevant entry and, sure enough, finds an explanation.

'Panda. Large black-and-white bear-like mammal, native to China. Eats, shoots and leaves.'

The book's popularity also shows that readers care about wayward punctuation such as that errant comma after "eats."

Take the much-abused apostrophe. That elegant little squiggle has only a few functions, yet it sometimes litters a patch of writing like shavings on a magnet.

As punctuation goes, the apostrophe is simple:

1) It marks the omitted letter or letters in a contraction. *It's* for *it is. Can't* for *cannot. They're* for *they are. I could've* danced all night. (*Could've* means could *have*, not could

"of." And *it's* can mean both *it is* — *it's* midnight — and *it has* — *it's* been a long time).

2) The apostrophe marks possession: *John's* desk. The *desk's* drawer. A whole *year's* work. Notice we could also say the desk *of* John, the drawer *of* the desk, the work *of* a whole year — "of" structures that show possession.

With a single owner, add an apostrophe and then S: John *Smith's* desk, *Sam's* dog. If the noun already ends in S, the most common style is to omit the additional S after the apostrophe: John *Williams'* pen.

Some stylebooks, however, depart from that treatment [*Williams'*] and add apostrophe-plus-S even to words already ending in S, making it *Williams's*. Neither style is wrong; the important thing is to *have* a style and stick to it, for consistency. (The influential *AP Stylebook* omits the additional S: John *Williams'* pen, and I follow AP style throughout this volume, as I did above when I wrote of Lynne *Truss'* book.)

When more than one person collectively owns an object, first make the owner(s) plural by adding S (or "es" to names that already end in S) and then an apostrophe: the *Bennetts'* house, the *Smiths'* car, the *Williamses'* house, the *Joneses'* car. Plural generic nouns ending in S need only an apostrophe: the *vampires'* fear of garlic, the *ducks'* quacking chorus.

When multiple people are listed as owners of an object, show joint ownership or possession by apostrophizing the final noun: *John and Mary's car, Sue and Sam's report*. But show separate ownership or possession with separate apostrophes: *John's and Mary's cars, Sue's and Sam's reports*. (Notice that the objects "owned" —

cars and reports — are plural with separate ownership, but singular with joint ownership.)

When the plural form of a word is spelled differently from the singular form, add apostrophe and S to both forms: *man's/men's, woman's/women's, child's/children's.*

3) The apostrophe marks the plural of letters, numerals, or symbols: *He was holding three 6's and a pair of 4's. She earned two A's and three B's. Mind your P's and Q's.* Apostrophes are usually omitted, however, when there is more than one letter or numeral: *They freed three POWs. He knows his ABCs. The airline bought a dozen new 727s. The roaring '20s* (note that an apostrophe marks the omitted "19" but not the plural S).

A couple of cautions. First, computer spelling and grammar checkers don't catch most errant apostrophes because such software looks for structural errors, misspellings, or words that are not in its dictionaries. A checker might flag all instances of *it's* and *its* and ask if it's the right one. Or it might catch some obvious error — "Mose's Law," for example, instead of "Moses' Law." But no checker can take the place of writer vigilance.

Second, apostrophe errors are everywhere, and the effect of constant error, especially on the young, is to confuse. The Internet is a showplace of misplaced apostrophes. Here's a sample from a bit of surfing:

Get *Your's* Now. Possessive pronouns have no apostrophes: *yours, ours, hers, his, theirs, its.*

A team of *chef's* will check each recipe to be sure of *it's* authenticity. Simple plural: *chefs.* "It's" is not possessive; it always means *it is* (or *it has*). "Its," on the other hand, is always possessive.

Check our website for a look at the many unwritten rules that *boss's* lay on their workers. Simple plural: *bosses.*

To all the ex-*Yankee's* that are homesick, check out this link. Simple plural: *Yankees.* (Also, for the record, that should be ex-Yankees *who* — not *that.* Ex-Yankees are human, too.)

If *your* a teacher, check this out & pass it on. This example appeared on a school district site, written by and for educators. We have teachers who don't know the contraction for *you are?* No wonder many students don't, either.

Huge Price *Reduction's* for *Womens*, *Mens* and *Childrens'* Clothing. How many mistakes can be made in nine words? This passage apostrophizes the simple plural *reductions,* skips the apostrophe on the possessives *women's and men's,* and puts an apostrophe in the wrong place in *children's.*

Writing *tool's* and other Writing *Requirement's.* If *Your* After A Bargain, *Its* Here! Another how-many-things-can-go-wrong entry. The plurals *tools* and *requirements* are wrongly apostrophized, and the possessive pronouns *your* and *its* should be *you're* and *it's.* (Let's not even mention the crazy capitalization.)

***Shoe's* Sale (Selected styles.)** What's the thinking here? Are the "selected styles" for just one foot?

Remember that stylebooks can vary on certain points. The best practice is to choose one dependable style guide and then to be consistent.

CHAPTER 46

GRAVEN ERRORS

The new Ground Zero cornerstone in New York City was laid with great fanfare, and it's unfortunate that the first thing that comes to mind when viewing it is that it's missing a comma. Those who put messages in stone should check their punctuation, spelling, and grammar before they start carving. The cornerstone should have been perfect, especially given the gravity and importance of its message. Instead, it displays a common mistake in punctuation: "To honor and remember those who lost their lives on September 11, 2001 and as a tribute to the enduring spirit of freedom."

There should be a comma after "2001." That comma is one of a *pair* of commas that sets off "2001" from the rest of the sentence.

Does it matter? It does. Do people care? They do. Consider the phenomenal popularity — first in Great Britain and now in the United States — of Lynne Truss' *Eats, Shoots and Leaves,* a book on punctuation. Truss is the editor who glues commas or apostrophes on a stick and raises that punctuation to its proper place on errant marquees or signs. Sticklers could do likewise with the new cornerstone. But it would have been easier to do it right in the first place. As it stands, that piece of granite documents for posterity not only the awful event of 9/11 but also our carelessness with the language.

The lesson we draw from that costly error is *always proofread your signs.* That's good advice whether the notice is in stone, paper, or wood. Too bad those posting this sign in a safari park didn't notice that it needed a period: "Elephants please stay in your cars."

Apostrophe errors abound, and it's no surprise they appear in signs as well. From a sign hawking sheepskin seat covers: "We know your hot!"

A reader sends the following: A Houston honky-tonk emblazons "Nigth Club" as part of its name. A road sign says: "Codstruction." A Florida juvenile agency sign includes the word "childern." A midway ride neon sign declares: "Fligth to Mars."

Consider the ubiquitous "BBQ" sign. No way that entrenched abbreviation is going to change, but it derives from a misspelling — there is no Q in "barbecue."

Omitting serial (or "Oxford") commas also causes sign problems. (The serial comma is the final comma before the "and" in a list, recommended by experts and indefensibly omitted only by journalists.) A restaurant sign: "Special today: grilled chicken, sloppy joe, BBQ and tunafish salad sandwiches." *Yum*: barbecued beef and tunafish salad on a bun. Placing a comma before the "and" clarifies: "Special today: grilled chicken, sloppy joe, BBQ, and tunafish salad sandwiches."

A reader sends another such screwy notice: "Door prizes will include lab equipment, books written by members of the bio department and a fruitcake." One of the authors is a fruitcake?

Consider this dedication: "To my parents, Gloria Steinem and Martin Luther King, Jr." (Now *there's* a story that hasn't been told.) To avoid suggesting that the parents were Gloria Steinem and Martin Luther King, Jr., the dedication should read: "To my parents, Gloria Steinem, and Martin Luther King, Jr."

Dangling modifiers often amuse, as illustrated by a laundromat sign posted over the washing machines: "Please remove all your clothes when the light goes out." Another from a sign posted at a conference: "For anyone who has children and doesn't know it, there is a day care on the first floor."

Careful proofreading also helps avoid bloopers:

- *Toilet out of order. Please use floor below.*
- *The most exclusive disco in town. Everyone welcome.*
- Sign on a health food store window: *Closed due to illness.*
- Notice on a church door: *This is the gate of heaven. Enter ye all by this door. (This door is kept locked because of the draft. Use side door.)*

Epitaph bloopers are forever. We've all seen such tombstone typos as "Rest in Piece," or "Born 1924, Diseased 1990," or "Now with the angles." Here's a memorable epitaph blooper:

The manner of his death was thus:
He was druv over by a bus.

CHAPTER **47**

LITTLE WORDS, BIG TROUBLE

You wouldn't think such little words as "a," "an," and "as" could cause much confusion, but they do. The chief problem with "a" and "an" is using "a" before a vowel sound or "an" before a consonant sound — "a eagle," "a incident," "an gratuity," or "an historic," for example.

Seems a small thing, but people grit their teeth just the same. It's a wonder that such mistakes with "a" and "an" happen at all, because the faulty form is harder to say than the correct form: an eagle, an incident, a gratuity, a historic. That's because vowel sounds glide effortlessly into consonant sounds, and vice versa, but they fight when butted against their own kind. Say aloud "an airplane" and "a airplane," and "a book" and "an book," and you'll hear what I mean.

Still, "an historic" or "an historical" is common diction. For example, the U.S. Navy resurrected a patriotic symbol when it directed its fleet to fly the red-and-white-striped "Don't Tread on Me" rattlesnake flag. Navy Secretary Gordon England said the flag would reflect the nation's determination in its war on terrorism because it represented "an historic reminder" of America's will to triumph.

"An historic" is not the preferred form because we

sound the beginning H, a consonant. Only when the H is silent do we correctly use "an": *an* heir, but *a* hair.

The problem with H words is more common when the stress falls on a second syllable — thus such phrasing as "an habitual criminal," "an hypothesis," or "an heroic." Although the H may be weak in such structures, it is not silent, and that settles the argument. As Bryan Garner writes in *Modern American Usage,* placing *an* before such words is "likely to strike readers and listeners as affectations." (The practice is probably more accepted in Great Britain; even so, R. W. Fowler, a leading authority on English usage, wrote nearly 80 years ago that British "opinion is divided" regarding H words with unstressed first syllables.)

A similar error is seen with the word *humble,* in which the H is also sounded. But the problem here is that some mispronounce the word — making it "umble." Thus, they say "an umble person" — observing the rule of using "an" before a vowel sound, but incorrectly using a vowel sound. I know of no dictionary whose preferred pronunciation for *humble* or *humbly* is "umble" or "umbly."

Sometimes people protest such phrasing as: "An FBI investigation that started the whole mess." Or "It's an NCAA policy." Or "She has an MA degree." They object that the article "an" is wrong because it precedes the consonants F, N, and M. But that's a misstatement of the rule. As we saw above, we use "a" before a consonant *sound* and "an" before a vowel *sound.* It's true that F, N, and M are consonants, and we would use "a" before the words *federal, national,* and *master's.* But here they are part of abbreviations, and they sound like "eff," "enn," and "emm."

Conversely, words beginning with vowels that sound like consonants take "a." Thus, it's *a eulogy* (the E sounds like Y), *a uniform* (the U sounds like Y), or *a Ouija* board (the O sounds like W). In the United States, it's *an herb* or *an herbal* (the H is silent), but *a herbicide* (the H is sounded).

American English made no clear distinction between "a" and "an" before the 1800s. The U.S. Constitution refers to "an uniform" rule of naturalization, for example. But for the last century at least, we've let the whole matter of "a" or "an" rest on pleasing the ear and tongue — it's as difficult to say "a hour" or "an history book" as it is unattractive to hear.

"As" is another little word that causes big trouble. For example, we often read or hear "as far as" without the words necessary to complete the thought: "As far as Williams' outside activity, the committee will disregard it." Accurate phrasing would render that sentence: "As far as Williams' outside activity *goes* [or *is concerned*], the committee will disregard it."

We can also repair such "as far as" structures by changing them to "as for": "As for Williams' outside activity, the committee will disregard it." (A tidier sentence, however, would be: "The committee will disregard Williams' outside activity.")

As often incorrectly follows such verbs as *named, called, elected*, etc.: "The association elected her *as* president." Or: "In high school, Jansen was named *as* the most likely to succeed." That's like saying: "The parents named their new baby *as* John." Omit *as*: "The association elected her president"; "In high school, Jansen was named most likely to succeed."

The ungrammatical "equally as" is yet another problem with that tiny word. A newspaper restaurant critic wrote that he liked the beef, but the veal was "equally as good." The veal was equally good, and that's what he should have written.

In careful writing, small things matter.

CHAPTER 48

SHORT AND CLEAR SAYS MORE

The overlong sentence is the equivalent of the weather: Everybody talks about it, but nobody does anything about it. Likewise, although everyone agrees that long sentences usually damage clarity and readability, they don't stop writing them.

Take this opening passage written by a veteran writer:

The retired four-star Army general who was sent to Iraq two weeks ago to assess operations there has concluded that American troops must speed up and strengthen the training of Iraqi security forces, by assigning thousands of additional military advisers to work directly with Iraqi units, said senior defense and military officials here and in Iraq.

The officer, Gen. Gary E. Luck, largely endorses a plan by American commanders in Iraq to shift the military's main mission after the Jan. 30 elections from fighting the insurgency to training Iraq's military and police forces to take over those security and combat duties and become more self-reliant, eventually allowing American forces to withdraw, the officials said.

If clear expression is an idea's most elegant dress, that writing is naked. It may serve certain journalistic precepts, but it doesn't serve the reader. And, unfortunately, it's all too typical. We're so used to such dense writing that we no longer see how bad it is.

But let's plead the reader's case and identify this writing for what it is. Read the passage aloud, and you'll hear at once what's wrong. First, it contains too many words to be clear. Its two sentences total 114 words — more than twice the optimal sentence length average of 25. The passage also is fussed up with prepositions, passive voice, and formula. Finally, it isn't conversational. It's bulky with artificial implants that may seem necessary to the writer — or to the editor, which amounts to the same thing — but not to the reader.

The looseness of overlong sentences allows poor phrasing as well: "The retired four-star Army general." The writer probably led with this vague identification because most readers would not recognize "Gen. Gary E. Luck." It's often sound to use a short generic label in the opening statement, holding specific identification for later — instead of an unrecognizable name or very long title. But a hefty six-word label that still fails to identify adds unnecessary weight to an already long sentence. A generic identification such as "retired general" or "military expert" (or officer, adviser, analyst) would be shorter, clearer, and less obtrusive.

"Was sent to Iraq two weeks ago to assess." That passive structure hides the actor. The active voice would have made it clear that Defense Secretary Donald Rumsfeld dispatched the general to Iraq, a meaningful detail buried in the story's 11th paragraph.

"Said senior defense and military officials here and in Iraq." Well, that's a bit much, isn't it? Here we are, trying to trim fat, and we waste 10 words on a meaningless attribution. Senior! Defense and military! Here and in Iraq! Too bad we can't say who they are!

Such language is journalese for "insiders you can trust." But readers *expect* the media to use sources they can trust. They don't want to be sidelined by unnecessary distinctions, nor will they parse a gummy sentence to capture coded significance. To readers, "officials" is clearer than "senior military and defense officials." If we can't name a source, fine, but we shouldn't bewilder the reader and burden the sentence with mysterious and useless clutter, either.

Prepositions and particles also clog the passage — a usual accompaniment to overlong sentences. Again, read the second sentence aloud, and see how its preposition and particle singsong damages flow and sense:

"The officer, Gen. Gary E. Luck, endorses a plan *by* American commanders *in* Iraq *to* shift the military's main mission *after* the Jan. 30 elections *from* fighting the insurgency *to* training Iraq's military and police forces *to* take over . . . ."

For conversational pacing, we want a wide variety of sentence lengths. But, everything being equal, clear writing tries for a sentence length average of about 25 words, as we suggested above. We must make room in the sentence for the vital message — especially in the lead. The story hangs upon action — actor, action, acted upon. Nonvital detail should be omitted or, if useful, included later in the story.

How might the passage above read if we rewrote it, using the writer's basic approach and style, but shortening, tightening, and clarifying? Can we add meaning by losing words? We can.

The United States must add thousands of advisers to work directly with Iraqi troops, concludes a military officer who analyzed the war effort in Iraq.

Gary E. Luck, a retired four-star Army general who conducted his two-week assessment for Defense Secretary Donald H. Rumsfeld, approves shifting the U.S. mission from fighting to training. The additional advisers would train Iraqi forces to assume security and combat duties after the Jan. 30 election, gradually allowing U.S. withdrawal.

That version cuts the original's 114 words to 75, yet it is immediately more informative because it's immediately clearer and more conversational.

CHAPTER 49

COMMON CONFUSIONS

A reader e-mails that a television ad for a fast food restaurant's new line of salads declares: "Each bite better than the *next!*" So, she says, the salad just tastes worse and worse the more you eat?

That ad writer's intended meaning was obviously: "Each bite better than the *last*."

That amusing faux pas shows how even professional writers get tangled in linguistic brambles when they don't pay attention to their words. Some mistakes show that we too readily copy others' expression without considering its accuracy. The following examples appeared in a television newscast, a novel, and a newspaper:

• "The police say if such a development occurs, they will know it *sooner than later*."

• "If he stayed on the island, he would be cornered *sooner than later*."

• "They say U.S. forces should leave *sooner than later*."

Who wants to be first to break it to those writers that "sooner than later" makes no sense? It's like saying "newer than older," or "fatter than thinner," or "easier than harder." "Sooner *or* later" is the obvious choice for the first two examples, and "sooner *rather* than later" would do for the third.

For some reason, the word *jibe* seems to bewilder even professional writers. One reporter writes that the details of a witness' account don't *gibe* with the official report. Another, covering the same story for another newspaper, writes that the two stories don't *jive*. Each should have written *jibe*, which means to be in accord or to agree. *Gibe* means to tease or taunt or joke. *Jive*, of course, is usually a kind of music or talk. The word also has other colloquial or slang meanings, but *jibe* isn't one of them.

Unfortunately, computer spell-checkers can't help with this kind of problem. Such software can't tell when we use the wrong word; it can only flag words that are not in its dictionary. If my typo spells something that happens to be in the spellchecker's dictionary, or if I confuse homonyms *(there, their, they're; to, too, two)*, the spellchecker will not flag my error. Ditto, the use of the wrong word: The spellchecker does not know that "gibe" is the wrong word; it only knows it is a word. Guess that's why it's called *artificial* intelligence.

The following passage illustrates another common confusion: "His education had *fortuitously* been in international economics, so when the company expanded, he was quickly pressed into service."

Now, his education in international economics may have been *fortunate*, given the circumstance of the company's expansion, but it was hardly fortuitous — people do not earn degrees by accident. *Fortuitous* means a chance occurrence or event — its synonym is *accidental*.

Here's the excellent writer P.D. James using the word "fortuitous" correctly in the opening of her novel *The Murder Room*:

On Friday 25 October, exactly one week before the first body was discovered at the Dupayne Museum, Adam Dalgliesh visited the museum for the first time. The visit was fortuitous, *the decision impulsive, and he was later to look back on that afternoon as one of life's bizarre coincidences.*

Some perhaps mistake *fortuitous* for a highfalutin version of *fortunate* because the words share a couple of syllables. But sharing syllable and sound is hardly an indicator of meaning. We don't suppose that *adventitious* means *adventurous*, or that *syllabub* means *syllabus*, or that *penumbra* means *penultimate*. (*Penultimate* itself is often misunderstood. It has nothing to do with quality or worth; it means next to last: The penultimate chapter in a 20-chapter book is Chapter 19.)

Here's a professional writer who doesn't know the difference between *milk toast* and *Milquetoast*: "His defensive approach to this crisis shows that he's nothing but a milktoast, an apologist rather than a leader."

That word should be spelled *Milquetoast,* which means a timid, meek, or unassertive person. The term comes from Caspar Milquetoast, a comic strip character created by cartoonist H.T. Webster in the 1920s. Caspar Milquetoast has been described as "a man who speaks softly and gets hit with a big stick." *Milk toast*, however, is a buttered toast, hot milk, and sugar concoction — which, as I recall from childhood, becomes increasingly sodden and slippery as you eat it. In other words: *Each bite better than the next!*

Chapter 50

Laying a Grammatical Egg

Do you see a basic but common grammatical error in the following sentence? "If nothing else, it lay the groundwork for a family-led public relations campaign to humanize Kenneth Lay."

That sentence, which appeared in a newspaper known for careful writing and editing, concerned an interview with Linda Lay, wife of former Enron chief Kenneth Lay. You probably immediately spotted the problem in "it lay the groundwork" — an unintentionally amusing *lie-lay* error in a story about a man named "Lay."

That sentence shows that the irregular verbs *lie* and *lay* can cause even careful writers and editors to lay an egg. But no need to lie low — the verbs aren't complicated, despite their frequent misuse. It helps to remember that TO LIE means to rest or recline, and TO LAY means to place or put something somewhere. (We'll ignore the forms of *lie* that mean to fib – that's a different word and causes no confusion.)

To clarify: The verb TO LIE includes *lie, lying, lay, have lain.* The verb TO LAY is even simpler: *lay, laying, laid, have laid.* The verb TO LIE does not have an object: The papers *lie* on the desk. The verb TO LAY has an object (place or put *something*): I'll *lay* the papers on the desk. The two verbs share a word, unhappily, which probably helps muddy the water. That shared word is *lay*, and it functions as the past tense of TO LIE (rest or recline) as well as the present tense of TO LAY (place or put). For example:

TO LIE (rest or recline): We will *lie* down today. We are *lying* down. We *lay* down yesterday. We have *lain* down every day this week.

TO LAY (place or put an object): We will *lay* bricks today. We are *laying* bricks. We *laid* bricks yesterday. We have *laid* bricks every day this week.

So back to that newspaper passage: The phrasing "it *lay* the groundwork" should have been "it *laid* the groundwork." It's a simple past-tense sentence using the verb TO LAY, meaning to place or put. (If the sentence were in present tense, it would read: "It lays the groundwork." Or, if the subject were plural, "They lay the groundwork.")

That's about as complicated as it gets. But before we lay this matter to rest — or let it lie — we should consider several other small hitches in the correct use of *lie* and *lay*. There is no *laid* in the verb *lie*. (And no "layed" anywhere — ever — despite that non-word's popularity.) So it is always wrong to say we "laid down" yesterday when we mean that we rested or reclined or *lay* down yesterday. One of the reasons this error is so common is that, in speech, a vowel preceding a consonant usually takes on the sound of the consonant. That means that even when we correctly say "lay down," it sounds the same as "laid down" because of the silent Y — the sounds merge, and "lay down" becomes "laiDown." Most blending or elision of sound causes few problems, and can even amuse. For example, "Did you eat yet?" can sound like "Jeet yet?" But in the case of "lay down," the merging of sound just happens to mimic a grammatical error.

Another problem is that we can become confused by such structures as "I'm going to lay my weary head on the pillow." We might be tempted to use *lie* because it seems we're talking about resting or reclining. But in this sentence's logic, my head is a direct object — I'm going to place or put it somewhere, same as I would a brick or a block of wood. (No jokes, please!)

A final note: Don't trust your computer's grammar or spell checker to catch lie and lay errors. Believe me, it doesn't have a clue. Throughout this column, my grammar checker made insane suggestions concerning the use of *lie* or *lay* — suggestions that would have made the work ungrammatical. Wonderful as such software is, it's a machine, and machines can't handle certain intricacies of language. That's one limit of *artificial* intelligence. Sometimes we need the real thing.

Chapter 51

Those Pesky Pronouns

If my mail from readers is any indication, solving our pronoun problems would also get rid of the grammar problems that bother people the most. Few gaffes generate as much heat as confusing subjective pronouns such as *I, he, she, we,* or *they* with objective pronouns such as *me, him, her, us,* or *them,* or using "-self" words as subjects or objects.

For example, a university professor says regarding the cost of the election per voter: "It bothers people inside the beltway and attentive watchers *like you and I* more than it does regular folks."

Another professor — oblivious of the irony in his own comment — says that the only people in his department who care about grammar "are two other instructors and *myself.*"

A newspaper columnist writes: "I notice that *you and her* have the same last name."

A TV home decorating show host says the new office makes "a wonderful workplace *for Sherry and I.*"

An editor says, "This is *between you and I,*" and a professional writer says, "They introduced the new director *to him and I.*"

An entertainment reporter says of a May/December

marriage: "She's at least 15 years older *than him.*"

A radio commentator says, "My wife has a better memory *than me.*"

Each of those examples is ungrammatical. It seems we all remember that it's wrong to say, "Johnny and me are going" — just as wrong as "me is going." It's wrong because we need a subject and *me* is an object. We naturally say, "I am going," but "Call me." We're so suspicious of "Johnny and me," however, that we may avoid it even when it's right. For example, we might say: *Call Johnny and I. Give it to Johnny and I. Tell Johnny and I.* If we take Johnny out of those sentences, though, we see how wrong "I" is — as wrong as *Call I; Give it to I; Tell I.*

The pronoun errors earlier in this column are just variations on the same theme. The pronoun we choose depends entirely upon whether it should be subject or object. If it's the actor (a subject), it should be *I, he, she, they, we, who.* If it's acted upon (an object), it should be *me, him, her, them, us, whom.*

"Self" pronouns are different from other pronouns because they are neither subjects nor objects, but reflexives (I hurt myself) or intensifiers (they are all going, but I myself am staying home). Again, if we would not say, "Myself is going," we likewise must not say, "John and myself are going." If we would not say, "Let myself know," we likewise must not say, "Let John or myself know."

Removing other people from the sentence and letting the pronoun in question stand alone quickly reveals which role the pronoun is playing — subject or object. And substituting other pronouns also can help in certain sentences. For example, if we know that it is right to say,

"This is between *us*," then we also know it is right to say, "This is between you and *me*" — because *us* is objective, and any pronoun we choose for this particular sentence would also have to be objective. "This is between you and *I*" is the same thing as "This is between *we*," and therefore wrong.

Pronouns in "than" sentences are easiest of all. If you can add a verb to the pronoun, and the sentence makes sense, choose the subjective pronoun: He's older than *I* [am]; I've been here longer than *she* [has]. We would not say older than me [am], been here longer than her [has], so the objective pronouns *me* and *her* are wrong in these structures.

Easy, eh? Yet problems with pronouns are a major source of verbal pollution, so it's nice to know that by resolving them, we can help clean up the linguistic environment overnight.

NOTES

NOTES

NOTES